THE PARDONER'S
PROLOGUE AND TALE

'The Gambler' from Holbein's *Dance of Death* (see p. v)

THE PARDONER'S PROLOGUE & TALE

FROM THE CANTERBURY TALES

BY

GEOFFREY CHAUCER

*Edited with Introduction, Notes
and Glossary by*

A. C. SPEARING

CAMBRIDGE
AT THE UNIVERSITY PRESS
1965

PUBLISHED BY
THE SYNDICS OF THE CAMBRIDGE UNIVERSITY PRESS

Bentley House, 200 Euston Road, London, N.W. 1
American Branch: 32 East 57th Street, New York, N.Y. 10022
West African Office: P.O. Box 33, Ibadan, Nigeria

©

CAMBRIDGE UNIVERSITY PRESS

1965

Printed in Great Britain at the University Printing House, Cambridge
(Brooke Crutchley, University Printer)

LIBRARY OF CONGRESS CATALOGUE
CARD NUMBER: 65-21782

CONTENTS

Note on the Frontispiece

The frontispiece is taken from Hans Holbein's *Dance of Death* (ed. J. M. Clark; Phaidon Press, London, 1947. Reproduced by courtesy of the Phaidon Press). It shows three gamblers, one of whom is being seized by Death and a devil. The plate is considerably later in date than *The Pardoner's Tale*; the motif of the Dance of Death is not known until the fifteenth century, and Holbein's version of it dates from the early sixteenth century. But it remains medieval in feeling, and this plate is extraordinarily close to the Tale in subject and in its restless violence of treatment.

ACKNOWLEDGEMENTS

The greatest tribute one can pay to scholarship is to make use of it. I have therefore, when writing about medieval pardoners in my Introduction, borrowed shamelessly and without detailed acknowledgement from 'Chaucer's Pardoner and the Pope's Pardoners' in part V of the Chaucer Society's *Essays on Chaucer* (1889) and *English Wayfaring Life in the Middle Ages* (2nd ed., London, 1889), both by J. J. Jusserand, and from *Some New Light on Chaucer* (London, 1926) by J. M. Manly. I am also, of course, much indebted throughout this edition to several of the poem's earlier editors, and I once again make no detailed acknowledgement of my debts. They are chiefly to F. N. Robinson's invaluable *The Complete Works of Geoffrey Chaucer* (2nd ed., Cambridge, Mass., 1957) and to the edition of *The Pardoner's Prologue and Tale* by Nevill Coghill and Christopher Tolkien (London, 1958). I am grateful, too, to Mr R. P. Hewett for making numerous and detailed comments on the whole book, and to Mr Maurice Hussey for suggesting a suitable illustration.

In various places I refer readers requiring further information or comment to *An Introduction to Chaucer*, by the three editors of this series of texts.

A. C. S.

Cambridge
January 1965

INTRODUCTION

The Pardoner's Tale is among those of *The Canterbury Tales* which have most often been extracted from the whole work and printed separately. It is right that this should be so, for it is certainly one of the finest of *The Canterbury Tales* and one of Chaucer's greatest works. The story itself, of three revellers who set out to kill Death and end by killing each other, is not original; nor are most of Chaucer's stories. This one is based on a folk-tale, of oriental origin, which has been found in various versions all over Europe. But it is told with a shattering intensity, and the emotion it arouses helps to convey a profound significance. It is turned into a story of damnation, in which we see the actors not simply judged by an outraged deity, but recklessly damning themselves, throwing themselves headlong upon their fate. It is difficult to think of another work in medieval English literature in which the actual *process* of damnation is presented with such horrifying force.

Much of this force, and much of the individual colouring of the actual tale, is drawn from its teller. Nearly all of the tales told on the pilgrimage to Canterbury are related to their tellers in some way. Sometimes the relationship is no more than a general appropriateness; this is the case with the Second Nun's pious Tale of a saint and martyr, for example, or with the Nun's Priest's delightful beast-fable[1]. But in other cases the tale told is made into an expression of the whole personality of the pilgrim who tells it, so that teller and tale are hardly separable, and the tale and all its

[1] For a different view of *The Nun's Priest's Tale*, see the edition by Maurice Hussey in this series.

surrounding material are fused into a dramatic monologue. This is true of *The Merchant's Tale*, of *The Wife of Bath's Tale* (where the Prologue is over twice as long as the Tale itself), and perhaps supremely of *The Pardoner's Tale*. The Pardoner can convey so full a sense of damnation in his Tale because he is himself on the edge of the pit, 'the one lost soul among the Canterbury pilgrims', as he has been called.[1] The Tale, like the Prologue, is self-revelatory; it exposes the nature of a consciousness which has cut all moral bearings and is veering with sick giddiness towards self-destruction. And yet this consciousness is itself set firmly in the everyday world. In Chaucer's Pardoner the common abuses of the age are shown as they really were, only with a poet's penetration into the human experience that lies behind historical documents. The setting is everyday in another sense, too. The Tale is dramatically related to the pilgrimage: it begins with an altercation among the pilgrims and comes to an end with another altercation. We are led from this world to the very brink of the next and then brought safely back. *The Pardoner's Tale* is a work of Chaucer's high maturity, dating probably from the last decade of his life, the thirteen-nineties, and undoubtedly written specifically for inclusion in *The Canterbury Tales* and for the Pardoner to tell. It shows Chaucer's poetic art at its height, extending itself under the urgent pressure of experience to a superb virtuosity.

In this Introduction, after a brief summary of the work's content, we shall be concerned first with the Pardoner himself and his historical background, and then, in order, with his Prologue, Tale and conclusion.

[1] G. L. Kittredge, *Chaucer and his Poetry* (Cambridge, Mass., 1915), p. 212.

Introduction

SUMMARY

3

THE PARDONER

We first meet the Pardoner long before he begins on his Tale, in *The General Prologue* to *The Canterbury Tales* (see Appendix). There the 'nine-and-twenty' men and women who gathered together at the Tabard Inn in Southwark before setting off on their pilgrimage to the shrine of St Thomas à Becket at Canterbury are described at varying lengths. Some are dismissed with a mere mention of their presence or with a brief description of only a few lines, but others are described in very great detail. The Pardoner is among these last. His description, which is quoted in full in the Appendix to this volume, is forty-six lines long. He is the last of all the pilgrims to be described, and he is placed in this position of emphasis as one of a pair. He and the Summoner, who is described at exactly equal length immediately before him, are presented as boon companions, riding together and singing in unison 'Com hider, love, to me'. This distinctly worldly song might seem inappropriate for two officers of the Church,

4

but it expresses accurately the nature of their devotion. Their hearts are in the world, and above all in the profit they can make for themselves out of their ecclesiastical function. This indeed is what we have come to expect of Chaucer's presentation of the Church: of the eight descriptions of ecclesiastical figures in *The General Prologue*, only one, that of the Parson, is unequivocally favourable, and that, in its generality and its reliance on denials of corruption ('He was a shepherde and *noght* a mercenarie'), seems to depict an ideal opposed to the reality of the times. The Summoner and the Pardoner are given far more detailed physical descriptions, the one red-faced and covered with hideous spots ('Of his visage children were aferd'), and the other effeminate, dressed in a ghastly parody of fashion, but with eyes staring like a hare's. Together they make a horrifying pair, whose loathsome outward appearance fully expresses their inner corruption. They have completely betrayed the trust placed in them by a Church which, in using them, was itself a traitor to its own ideals.

Pardoners in the medieval Church

The function of a pardoner in the medieval Church will require some explanation. Punishments were imposed on members of the Church for their sins, and these 'penances' might take various forms, such as repeating prayers or psalms, fasting, or other forms of self-mortification. Gradually the practice grew up of allowing sinners to exchange one form of punishment for another, and particularly of allowing them to pay a fine instead of performing a physical penance. By the fourteenth century the theory known as the Treasury of Grace had developed. According to this, the Church was the guardian of the merits of Christ, the Virgin, and the saints. Their merits were more than enough to compensate for all the sins that mankind might commit, and so it was possible for the Church, as keeper of the Treasury, to distribute them among its members. Thus individual penance came to seem unnecessary: all that was needed was true penitence and payment in money or goods. Thus the sinner would be dispensed from his penance, and the Church would obtain resources for carrying out good works.

Special officers were required for carrying out such exchanges: they were called *quaestores* in Latin, pardoners in English. They might be priests or monks, but they might also, like Chaucer's Pardoner, be laymen employed as professionals.[1] Their work would be carefully regulated by the higher authorities of the Church; they would require written authorization, signed and sealed by a bishop or by the pope himself; they would be allowed to remit the punishments only of those who were truly penitent, and their gains would have to be handed over to their superiors. This is what pardoners originally had been, and what they still ought to have been; but if we turn from this summary to the pardoner Chaucer describes, we find not a replica but an appalling parody.

Certain elements remain. A *quaestor* needed an episcopal licence, and Chaucer's Pardoner has not just

---

[1] There is no mention of the Pardoner's being in orders, and some evidence against it. He does not wear his hair tonsured, as a priest had to, but hanging spread out over his shoulders. And he interrupts *The Wife of Bath's Prologue* to assert that he 'was aboute to wedde a wyf'—a vain boast, no doubt, but one that a priest would be unlikely to make.

one but several, with the seals of all possible authorities
dangling from them:

> First I pronounce whennes that I come,
> And thanne my bulles shewe I, alle and some.
> Oure lige lordes seel on my patente,
> That shewe I first, my body to warente,
> That no man be so boold, ne preest ne clerk,
> Me to destourbe of Cristes hooly werk.
> And after that thanne telle I forth my tales.
> Bulles of popes and of cardinales,
> Of patriarkes and bishopes I shewe. (49–57)

He might possibly have had a genuine licence from 'oure
lige lord', the local bishop, but only the very simple could
expect him to be authorized as well by 'popes', 'cardinales', 'patriarkes' and 'bishopes'. These other documents
must surely be fakes, intended to dazzle the impression-
able. The Pardoner is careful to point out that he can offer
no help to those who have on their consciences sins so
appalling that they have not dared to confess them:

> Goode men and wommen, o thing warne I yow:
> If any wight be in this chirche now
> That hath doon sinne horrible, that he
> Dar nat for shame of it yshriven be,
> Or any womman, be she yong or old,
> That hath ymaad hir housbonde cokewold,
> Swich folk shal have no power ne no grace
> To offren to my relikes in this place.
> And whoso findeth him out of swich blame,
> He wol come up and offre in Goddes name,
> And I assoille him by the auctoritee
> Which that by bulle ygraunted was to me. (91–102)

But this apparent scrupulosity is really a lever for his own
advantage, for naturally none of his audience will wish to
admit publicly that his (or her) conscience is burdened in

this way. Instead, they will all come rushing forward with their offerings simply to prove that they are not in mortal sin. Moreover, though the Pardoner reminds his audience that they must have confessed their 'sinne horrible' before he will release them from their penance, he goes on to claim that he will then *assoille* (absolve) them. He makes the claim more explicit at the end of his Tale, when he turns immediately to his audience in order to exploit the story's effect on their emotions:

> Now, goode men, God foryeve yow youre trespas,
> And ware yow fro the sinne of avarice!
> Myn hooly pardoun may yow alle warice,
> So that ye offre nobles or sterlinges,
> Or elles silver broches, spoones, ringes.
> Boweth youre heed under this hooly bulle!
> Cometh up, ye wives, offreth of youre wolle!
> Youre names I entre heer in my rolle anon;
> Into the blisse of hevene shul ye gon.
> I yow assoille by myn heigh power,
> Yow that wol offre, as clene and eek as cleer
> As ye were born.   (618–29)

> Looke which a seuretee is it to yow alle
> That I am in youre felaweshipe yfalle,
> That may assoille yow, bothe moore and lasse,
> Whan that the soule shal fro the body passe.   (651–4)

Clearly he is claiming the power to absolve sinners not only from the penance for their sins (*a poena*) but also from the sins themselves (*a culpa*). He is offering to *warice* (cure) them from the effect of sin, to restore them to the innocence of a newly born child, to send them straight to heaven at the moment of death; but these powers belonged only to a priest, not to a lay *quaestor*. The Pardoner's constant trick is to usurp the role of a priest, and to exploit it for histrionic purposes—it is the role

8

itself that he finds attractive and profitable, not the responsibilities that should go with it.

> I stonde lyk a clerk in my pulpet (105)

he says; and preaching is another of the priest's powers that he lays claim to. His whole offering to the pilgrims is in the form of a specimen sermon, with the Tale itself as an illustration of his text; but lay *quaestores* were in general specifically prohibited from preaching.

With the role of priest he combines that of medicine-man or witch-doctor. The trappings he makes most play with are spurious holy relics, with the power (as he says) to work miracles. Among those mentioned in *The General Prologue* are the veil of the Blessed Virgin (actually a pillow-case) and a piece of the sail from St Peter's boat. Later we hear of the transparent cases

> Ycrammed ful of cloutes and of bones (62)

which will heal and protect men and beasts, and even cure jealousy; of a mitten which will ensure a good crop to anyone who has put his hand in it; and of other relics, of unspecified power, available for kissing by the faithful if a suitable offering is made. All this is little different from a claim to magical powers, and though it does not take in Harry Bailly, the Host, it is evidently effective among the Pardoner's usual audiences, for he claims to make a hundred marks a year by his 'craft'. Here a last difference from the *quaestor* as he should be emerges. The true *quaestor* collects money for the Church, but the Pardoner keeps all he gains for his own profit, and indeed boasts of the fact. The constant theme of his preaching is ˙

> Ware yow fro the sinne of avarice (619)

but avarice is his own ruling passion. He is aware of the paradox, and calls it constantly to our attention.[1]

Evidence about Fourteenth-Century Pardoners

How are we to explain this vast difference between the *quaestor* according to the canons of the Church and Chaucer's Pardoner? We may feel tempted to suppose that Chaucer was simply inventing an anti-ecclesiastical satire to shock his audience and make them laugh. But historical evidence shows that in the Pardoner he has drawn an astonishingly accurate picture of the *quaestor* as he really was in the fourteenth century. The original idea of the office had become utterly corrupted, and historical warrant can be found for every aspect of the corruption that Chaucer depicts.

In 1390—only a few years before the probable date of composition of *The Pardoner's Tale*—Pope Boniface IX issued a letter in which he exposed some of the very abuses presented by Chaucer. There are false pardoners, he says, who 'affirm that they are sent by us or by the legates or nuncios of the apostolic see, and that they have been given a mission...to receive money for us and the Roman Church, and they go about the country under these pretexts'. Chaucer's Pardoner similarly claims to come from Rome, and the 'simple' pilgrim Chaucer of *The General Prologue* swallows his claim unquestioningly:

> With him ther rood a gentil Pardoner
> Of Rouncivale, his freend and his compeer,
> That streight was comen fro the court of Rome.
>
> His walet lay biforn him in his lappe,
> Bretful of pardoun, comen from Rome al hoot.

[1] See below, pp. 18, 26, for further consideration of this paradox.

The Pardoner is presented not only as having come from Rome, but as being 'of Rouncivale'—that is to say, as being employed to collect alms by the Chapel and Hospital of Our Lady of Rouncivalle at Charing Cross, just outside London. He may really have held this position, but there are grounds for suspicion, because in the thirteen-eighties warrants were issued to arrest persons claiming to be collecting alms for the Rouncivalle Hospital but converting their receipts to their own use. Once again Chaucer is following historical fact. Boniface goes on in his letter that these false *quaestores* 'proclaim to the faithful and simple people the real or pretended authorizations which they have received; and, irreverently abusing those which are real, in pursuit of infamous and hateful gain, they carry further their impudence by mendaciously attributing to themselves false and pretended authorizations of this kind'. We have just seen how Chaucer's Pardoner displays his many 'bulles' in this way; and Chaucer follows Pope Boniface in leaving us in doubt as to whether they were 'real or pretended authorizations'. Boniface was right in thinking forgery likely; in 1378 a certain 'Thomas Pardoner' was arrested as a 'forger of the seal of the Lord the Pope'.

Chaucer's Pardoner offers absolution *a poena et a culpa*; and there are documents to show that in this too he was only following the practice of the time. In 1340 the bishop of Durham issued a warning against pretended *quaestores* who 'absolve the perjured, homicides, usurers, and other sinners who confess to them; and, on receipt of a little money, grant remission for ill-atoned crimes'. In 1369 Pope Urban V wrote to the archbishop of Canterbury, also complaining of *quaestores* in England who sold absolution *a poena et a culpa*. Chaucer's Pardoner, in his greed, is willing to accept goods instead of money in payment for his services:

> Myn hooly pardoun may yow alle warice,
> So that ye offre nobles or sterlinges,
> Or elles silver broches, spoones, ringes.   (620–2)

In this too he seems to be typical, for the bishop of Durham orders false *quaestores* to be arrested and deprived of 'the money *and any other articles* collected by them'. The preaching activities of the Pardoner are fully parallelled in fourteenth-century documents; indeed, Pope Urban spoke of *quaestores* who usurped the pulpit from the parish priest, prevented him from celebrating mass, and collected the offerings themselves. It was perhaps in this way that the Pardoner

> whan that he fond
> A povre person dwellinge upon lond,
> Upon a day he gat him moore moneye
> Than that the person gat in monthes tweye.

The use of relics as miracle-working and profit-producing devices was extremely common in the Middle Ages. It was by no means confined to *quaestores*—far more august persons were also involved—but Chaucer seems hardly to have exaggerated at all in describing his Pardoner's monstrous deceptions. St Peter's sail and Our Lady's veil are no more improbable—perhaps less—than St Peter's vest (for which King Edward III in 1363 had paid 100*s*.) and some of Our Lady's milk (which was shown to pilgrims at Walsingham).

The poetic effect of Chaucer's Pardoner

It seems, then, that, grotesquely exaggerated as Chaucer's
Pardoner may appear, his way of life was in fact that of a
possible, if not typical, *quaestor* of the fourteenth century.
But to defend Chaucer against the charge of distorting
historical truth is not to say very much about his *poetic*
achievement in *The Pardoner's Prologue and Tale*. Chaucer
was by no means the only writer of his time to present a
pardoner unfavourably. William Langland, notably,
writing at the same time as Chaucer, though in alliterative
verse, not rhyme, emphasizes in his *Piers Plowman* the
difference between God's pardon and the 'pardon' that is
simply a matter of words, and gives a satirical description of
a *quaestor* which follows exactly the same lines as Chaucer's:

> There prechide a pardoner as he a prest were;
> Broughte forth a bulle with bisshopis selis
> And seide that hymself mighte assoile hem alle
> Of falsnesse of fastyng and of avowes broken.
> Lewide men levide hym wel and likide his speche;
> Comen up knelynge to kissen his bulle.
> He bunchede hem with his brevet and bleride here eiyen
> And raughte with his rageman ryngis and brochis.[1]

A pardoner preached there as if he were a priest; he brought
out a licence with bishops' seals on it, and said that he had
power to absolve them all for breaking fasts or vows.
Ignorant men believed him and liked what he said; they
came up on their knees to kiss his licence. He thrust his
letter of indulgence in their faces and bleared their eyes
and with his charter seized rings and brooches.

This offers the same evidence as Chaucer, even down to the
detail of the 'ryngis and brochis' that are accepted instead

[1] *Piers Plowman: The A Version*, ed. George Kane (London, 1960),
Prologue, 65–72.

of money. One might almost believe that Langland and Chaucer were describing the same man. But Langland's stern and laconic analysis has a quite different effect on us from Chaucer's treatment of the same material, and it is this effect with which we must now concern ourselves, if we wish to understand what Chaucer has to offer us that cannot be found in pontifical or archiepiscopal letters or anywhere else at all.

The effect the Pardoner has on us, as Chaucer describes him in *The General Prologue*, is at once comic, contemptible, and sinister. The comedy is not purely satirical; it does not preclude enjoyment in its object, and in this it is very typical of Chaucer. Through him, we can delight in the roguery of a thoroughgoing rogue, and so we can take pleasure in the details of the Pardoner's trickery—the pillow-case which is supposed to be Our Lady's veil, the 'pigges bones' which serve for holy relics, and the special skill he puts into singing an 'offertorie'.

But through this delight runs a strong vein of contempt, which surfaces not so much in his actions as in his physical appearance. He rides along as a ghastly parody of a fashionable young man, with his hood left off 'for jolitee' and his yellow hair spread out over his shoulders. But the hair is lank and thin, and the scorn leaps out in Chaucer's 'Him thoughte he rood al of the newe jet'— he rode along in the very latest fashion (in his own opinion). He is a parody not just of fashion but of manhood:

> A voys he hadde as smal as hath a goot.
> No berd hadde he, ne nevere sholde have;
> As smothe it was as it were late shave.
> I trowe he were a gelding or a mare.

The essential fact underlying all this outward display is brought out in the last line, in the blunt language of the farmyard: either he has lost his virility, or else he never possessed it.

Modern scholarship has shown how exactly the Pardoner's physical features reproduce those which medieval physiology assigned to the eunuch—the beardlessness, the high bleating voice, the long hair in which he takes such pride, the long neck implied in his self-description in his Prologue—

> Thanne peyne I me to strecche forth the nekke,
> And est and west upon the peple I bekke,
> As dooth a dowve sittinge on a berne   (109-11)

—and the staring eyes mentioned in *The General Prologue*: 'Swiche glaringe eyen hadde he as an hare'.[1] These signs of physical sterility may act as images of a different kind of sterility—the spiritual emptiness disclosed in his Prologue and Tale. This is perhaps one reason why Chaucer chose to make his Pardoner a eunuch. But they also have a more direct effect, in arousing repulsion and even fear. Sexual power the Pardoner may lack—his interjection about taking a wife in *The Wife of Bath's Prologue* is only an ineffective blind. But he possesses a power which is far greater and far more sinister—a power over men's souls, arising not from any physical advantages but from his will alone. That such a weakly impotent creature—so different from other rogues among the pilgrims, such as the Shipman with his beard, his brown complexion and his dagger, or even the Summoner with his 'fyr-reed cherubinnes face'— that such a creature should possess such power to make

---

[1] W. C. Curry, *Chaucer and the Mediaeval Sciences* (2nd ed., London, 1960), pp. 54-70.

men act as he wishes: there is something sinister in that. The sinister remains a fundamental element when the Pardoner begins on his Prologue and Tale.

THE PARDONER'S PROLOGUE

After being described in *The General Prologue*, the Pardoner, as we have seen, makes one or two interjections while the Wife of Bath is speaking, but his main contribution to the pilgrimage comes after *The Physician's Tale*. The Physician has told a gloomy story of sin and retribution, concerning a wicked magistrate's attempt to misuse the law in order to seduce the beautiful and virtuous daughter of a knight. He is prevented by her father's killing her to save her from the magistrate's power, and the magistrate in turn is cast into prison and commits suicide. The Host is much affected by this story. His feelings, whether sympathetic or contemptuous, are aroused as readily by fiction as by reality; and, after lamenting and moralizing over this sad story for a while, he declares that he needs some remedy for his grief— either one provided by the Physician himself, or something to drink, or a more cheerful story. He therefore calls on the Pardoner to 'Telle us som mirthe or japes right anon'. The Pardoner agrees without hesitation, only saying that he must first stop at an inn the pilgrims are just passing, in order to have a drink and a snack. But at this the 'gentils' among the pilgrims—those of higher social class and hence of more refined tastes (such as, presumably, the Knight and the Prioress)—hastily cry out that the Pardoner must not tell them 'ribaudye' but 'som moral thing'. It is obvious from the Pardoner's appearance and behaviour that he is a rogue, who might be expected to tell a grossly indecent story; and, since he is proposing to take a drink first, the 'gentils' have reason to be worried at the thought of what impropriety he might produce once drunk. Perhaps surprisingly, he agrees at once to the demand of the 'gentils', but still says that he must pause and drink while he is thinking of 'som honest thing'.

At this stage, presumably, we may imagine the pilgrims gathered round in the tavern to listen to what the Pardoner has to say, though at what point, if any, the journey towards Canterbury is resumed is not clear. Some readers of *The Pardoner's Tale* have been convinced that the whole narrative is delivered in the tavern, and since the Tale itself is about three drunken revellers, there would be a certain appropriateness in that. But since Chaucer provides no indication of the setting whatever, and does not even indicate whether the pilgrims are riding or resting, the setting can hardly be of much importance. We may visualize it as we choose. Instead of starting straight away on his 'honest' Tale, the Pardoner begins reminiscing about his own technique as a preacher. Reminiscence passes imperceptibly into demonstration, and back into reminiscence; he harangues the pilgrims as if they were his congregation, and then explains that he was only acting a part. Lastly, in detail and with vigour, he expounds his own motives in his preaching: partly malice, but fundamentally avarice. Now much of the detail the Pardoner supplies about his techniques is, as we have seen, perfectly accurate historically. The display first of impressively sealed documents and then of rags and bones which he calls relics; the monstrous claims he makes for the miraculous powers of these relics; the assertion that he has authority to absolve all who make offerings to them: all this is thoroughly realistic.

But at first sight it may be difficult to explain in realistic terms his exposure of his own motives. He admits that his technique is a *gaude* (trick), a matter of *false japes* (deceiving lies), intended solely to make his audience free in giving him money. With devastating bluntness, he remarks that

> . . .myn entente is nat but for to winne,
> And nothing for correccioun of sinne.
> I rekke nevere, whan that they been beried,
> Though that hir soules goon a-blakeberied. (117–20)

He repeats the same assertion of motive, and himself points out the paradox that he supplies his own avarice by preaching against the avarice of others:

> But shortly myn entente I wol devise:
> I preche of no thing but for coveitise.
> Therfore my theme is yet, and evere was,
> *Radix malorum est Cupiditas.*
> Thus kan I preche again that same vice
> Which that I use, and that is avarice. (137–42)

He ends his prologue with a confident elaboration on his intentions, the blatant assertion of a will directed towards material success:

> What, trowe ye that whiles I may preche,
> And winne gold and silver for I teche,
> That I wol live in poverte wilfully?
> Nay, nay, I thoghte it nevere, trewely!
> For I wol preche and begge in sondry landes;
> I wol nat do no labour with mine handes,
> Ne make baskettes, and live therby,
> By cause I wol nat beggen idelly.
> I wol noon of the apostles countrefete;
> I wol have moneie, wolle, chese, and whete,

Al were it yeven of the povereste page,
Or of the povereste widwe in a village,
Al sholde hir children sterve for famine.
Nay, I wol drinke licour of the vine,
And have a joly wenche in every toun. (153-67)

In this passage the assertion of will is enacted in the
seven-times repeated 'I wol' and in the scathing annihila-
tion of the conventional prejudices the Pardoner attributes
to his listeners: 'What, trowe ye...? ...Nay, nay...'.
The will's object is present in the unashamedly specific
'moneie, wolle, chese, and whete' and 'joly wenches'. The
last are presumably, in view of his lack of virility, an idle
boast; but that is beside the point.

Realism and convention in the Pardoner's confession

But why, it may be asked, does the Pardoner disclose his
aims and intentions in this way? Surely it would pay him
to keep quiet about his villainy, and allow himself to
appear as a preacher whose purpose is to save souls, not
line his purse? His boasting about his avarice seems to
undermine his means of satisfying it. Such an objection is
based partly on a misunderstanding of Chaucer's art. On
the surface it is highly realistic, so realistic that it may
deceive us into supposing that what it offers is actual
reality, a slice of life itself. But Chaucer's realism of detail
is usually only a technique, employed to supply insights and
pleasures that total realism cannot achieve. *The Wife of
Bath's Prologue* is an outstanding example. The Wife, by
way of introduction to her Tale, tells us the whole story
of her married life and the philosophy of sex and marriage
she has deduced from her varied experience. (She has had
no fewer than five husbands, and has fought with all of

them.) As she speaks we seem to be hearing the very voice of a vigorous uneducated woman, mesmerized in her reminiscences by the concrete detail of experience, and losing her way among digressions just as any real person might:

> But now, sire, lat me se, what shal I seyn?
> A ha! by God, I have my tale ageyn.

But if we look below this realistic surface, we see that the material of her Prologue, anecdotal and moralizing, is drawn from a whole collection of learned sources in Latin and French, by authors as various as Theophrastus, St Jerome, Walter Map and Eustache Deschamps, whom it is quite impossible that a 'real' Wife of Bath could have read (though she may have heard their arguments from the scholar among her husbands). In this way, Chaucer can provide at the same time the vigorous sexuality and appetite for experience which are expressed in the Wife's realism of speech, and argument on the question of marriage itself far more searching than anything an actual Wife of Bath would have thought of. There is a disparity between the spontaneous surface and the learned core, but surface and core co-operate to achieve a more powerful effect than either could gain separately. A parallel may be found in the medieval visual arts. There, too, realism of detail is frequently combined with formality of structure. In a famous *Pietà* by Rogier van der Weyden, for example, the detailed surface of things is minutely realistic—the texture of cloth and the folds it falls in, or the horrifyingly lifelike wounds on Christ's body—and yet the body as a whole is depicted quite unrealistically in both posture and proportions, in a way which expresses the pathos and anguish of the event far more vividly than realism could do.

Similarly in *The Pardoner's Prologue*. On the surface lie details so accurate that we can verify them from historical sources. But beneath them we find an 'unrealistic' literary convention, that of the confession. In real life people do not usually expound their own bad motives with the freedom that the Pardoner uses. Chaucer might allow these motives to appear gradually and surreptitiously from beneath a hypocritical front, but that strategy would require the diffuse development of the novel to be fully effective. In a short, concentrated work such as *The Pardoner's Prologue and Tale*, the Pardoner's true motives can best be revealed directly by himself in a confession to all who care to listen. Such confessions are extremely common in earlier medieval literature, and the Pardoner's is probably related to the confession of Fauxsemblant (False Seeming) in the *Roman de la Rose*, a thirteenth-century French poem which had been translated by Chaucer at an early stage of his literary career. There the speaker of the confession is a personification, who is not supposed to be lifelike, and the confession is simply a dramatic means of exposing the operations of deception in the world. Hence there is not the discrepancy found in *The Pardoner's Prologue* between realism and conventionalism. In *The Pardoner's Prologue* such a discrepancy does exist, but, once one understands why, it is easy to disregard it and accept willingly the other advantages it makes possible.

When all this has been said, however, one might still feel dissatisfied with an explanation of the confessional element in *The Pardoner's Prologue* solely in terms of convention. For one thing, the Pardoner's confession has been given a realistic ground in the pause to take a drink—

if he is not exactly drunk, his tongue has at least been loosened by 'a draughte of corny ale'. Again, he is not before his usual congregation of 'lewed peple', but before a temporary audience of pilgrims to whom he is giving a demonstration and perhaps feels that he can afford to expose himself. But there is a more fundamental consideration than these. The fact is that a great deal of the poem's force is directly derived *from* the confessional element itself, not achieved *in spite of* that element. If we read *The Pardoner's Prologue* responsively, giving ourselves up to Chaucer's imaginative world without troubling about probability, there is no question of simply *accepting* a convention: we are carried away by the force of the Pardoner's self-exposure. In that self-exposure lies his power over all his audiences—his congregations, the pilgrims, and ourselves. An essential feature of the evil embodied in the Pardoner is that it should be self-confident, blatant, the very opposite of ashamed of itself. The Pardoner does not simply 'confess' his wickedness, but thrusts it upon the pilgrims, and re-enacts it with the irresistible power of an actor—an actor, as it were, playing himself. This self-dramatization is the secret of his success as a preacher: it is a triumph of the will projecting itself outwards in threat, denunciation, or seductive whisper, and absorbing its audience's will, as well as their money, into itself. The Pardoner glories in the power he possesses, and characterizes it metaphorically in the repeated image of a poisonous snake:

Thanne wol I stinge him with my tonge smerte.... (127)

Thus spitte I out my venym under hewe
Of hoolinesse....   (135–6)

22

This image draws its power not only from common experience but from Scriptural tradition: the Psalmist says of his enemies: 'They have sharpened their tongues like serpents; adders' poison is under their lips' (Psalm cxl. 3). The snake, moreover, is supposed to hypnotize its victims by staring at them. Similarly, the Pardoner, at least when dealing with the pilgrims, does not pretend to be virtuous or altruistic, but fixes them with his 'glaringe eyen' and draws them into his own evil. This evil arouses horror, certainly, but it also arouses fascination, and a fascination which has nothing to do with sympathy. One scholar has written that the Pardoner 'is to be pitied rather than censured',[1] but surely pity and censure are both lost in this strange fusion of fascination and horror.

The art of preaching

The Pardoner, then, is irresistibly self-assertive. But he presents himself in the role of a preacher, and self-assertive is exactly what a preacher ought not to be. In the Middle Ages, and indeed down to the eighteenth or nineteenth century, the sermon was one of the most important literary forms, and much thought was given to its construction. This thought was embodied in the Middle Ages in an elaborate theory of preaching, the *ars praedicandi* (art of preaching). Many works on the art of preaching (*artes praedicandi*) were written in England in the thirteenth and fourteenth centuries, and there can be little doubt that Chaucer would have been familiar with their doctrines, if only from hearing many sermons preached. Their doctrines are extremely complex, but for our

---

[1] Curry, *Chaucer and the Medieval Sciences*, p. 70.

purpose they may be divided into two parts, moral and technical.

According to the moral part of the medieval *ars praedicandi*, the preacher is a mouthpiece for the Holy Spirit. He is genuinely inspired, and must follow God's guidance rather than any human art. Above all, he must preach not in order to show off himself and his skill but in order to praise God and to teach and improve his neighbours. The Pardoner's aim in preaching is thus a total perversion of the *ars praedicandi* as it should be. On the other hand, he is immensely skilled in the technical part of the *ars*. The *artes praedicandi* teach an enormously complicated rhetoric, according to which the preacher's text is divided into three parts, each supported by a further Scriptural reference; these three parts may then be further subdivided and Scripturally 'confirmed', and so on. The whole sermon is linked together by verbal 'correspondences', embellished with figures of rhetoric and illustrative stories, and turned into a public meditation on the original text with a structure as complex as that of a sonata or a symphony.

The Pardoner does not follow this structure in any detail, but he makes virtuoso use of many of the techniques of preaching. The *theme* round which his whole sermon is elaborated is *Radix malorum est cupiditas* (St Paul's 1st Epistle to Timothy, vi. 10: 'The love of money is the root of all evils'), and he illustrates this *theme* with many *ensamples* (Latin *exempla*, specific incidents used to ram home a general assertion). Some of these are taken from the Bible, some from secular writers, some from everyday life; and the Tale itself is an *exemplum* told to illustrate the *theme*. The style of his sermon is made

more dramatic by such appealing rhetorical figures as apo-
strophe—

> O wombe! O bely! O stinking cod!   (248)

—and onomatopoeia—'Sampsoun, Sampsoun!' (268) as
an imitation of a drunkard's heavy breathing. All these
devices are used frequently in the preaching section at the
beginning of the Tale, then cut down while the actual
story is being told, and brought back with renewed force
once the story is ended.

The Pardoner also makes brilliant use of those spell-
binding techniques that can be learned only from experience, not from any formal art: the manipulation of
suspense, climax, and anti-climax; the modulation from
one tone of voice to another; the alternation of simplicity
and complexity; and so on. His whole performance—it *is*
a performance, a histrionic achievement—is extraordinarily
accomplished. What is more, it works, not simply in
exploiting its listeners' emotions, but in creating a genuine
sense of horror at the sin it is directed against, and of
terror at God's vengeance on the sinners. The Pardoner is
perverting the preacher's art, and yet achieving an effect
even more powerful than the true preacher (of whose work
Chaucer provides us with a specimen in the long, meticu-
lously constructed, and tedious *Parson's Tale*). The
Pardoner is perfectly aware of this paradox. It was indeed
a commonplace of the times, and in stating it Chaucer
borrows again from the *Roman de la Rose*:

> For certes, many a predicacioun
> Comth ofte time of yvel entencioun;
> Som for plesance of folk and flaterye,
> To been avaunced by ypocrisye,
> And som for veyne glorie, and som for hate. (121-5)

As applied by the Pardoner, this paradox has two aspects. One is that he preaches against avarice out of avarice and yet genuinely succeeds in deterring people from avarice:

> Thus kan I preche again that same vice
> Which that I use, and that is avarice.
> But though myself be gilty in that sinne,
> Yet kan I maken oother folk to twynne
> From avarice, and soore to repente. (141–5)

The other aspect is that though he is himself 'vicious', he can still tell a 'moral tale'—a tale all the more effective because he *is* 'vicious', and can evoke from experience the sin he is preaching against:

> For though myself be a ful vicious man,
> A moral tale yet I yow telle kan,
> Which I am wont to preche for to winne. (173–5)

The nature of this 'moral tale' we must now consider.

THE PARDONER'S TALE

The actual story the Pardoner tells, as has already been mentioned, is not original. A basic plot concerning two or three men who find some treasure, disregard a wise man's warning that it will cause death, and plan simultaneously to kill each other for it by poison and violence, is widely distributed throughout Europe in the Middle Ages. Like many medieval popular tales, it is probably of oriental origin—a primitive version is found in a third-century Buddhist text, the *Jatakas*—but the version closest to Chaucer's is in an Italian work of 1572, the *Libro di Novelle e di Bel Parlar Gentile*. This is too late to have been Chaucer's source, and in fact we do not know where Chaucer got his version of the Tale, or how much he added to it. The mysterious old man whom the revellers in

The Pardoner's Tale meet, and who is himself seeking death, appears to be adapted from the wise man (a philosopher or hermit) who gives a warning against the treasure as a cause of death. Neither his quest for death nor that of the three revellers appears in any of the known parallels to the story, and it seems likely that the whole theme of the quest for death was added by Chaucer. The old man who wishes to die is not original, however. He seems to have been borrowed by Chaucer from an elegy by Claudian, and may also have been influenced by the legend of the Wandering Jew, who was supposed to be condemned never to die. However, these questions of origin, fascinating though they are for their own sake, are not particularly relevant to Chaucer's own achievement in *The Pardoner's Tale*. Medieval writers, unlike modern novelists, did not normally invent their own stories. They preferred to make use of stories which already existed— often stories which had been passed on by word of mouth without the intervention of writing—and then to combine and modify these so as to adapt them to their own pur- poses. Chaucer, in *The Canterbury Tales*, though not in his earlier work, appears sometimes to borrow stories from oral tradition in this way, and his 'source' in such a case will naturally remain unidentifiable. The actual experience which Chaucer conveys in *The Pardoner's Tale*, though it may have been suggested to him by various sources, can be shared only by a sensitive response to the Tale itself.

The discourse on the sins

The Pardoner's Tale falls clearly into two parts. One is the actual story, and the other is a discourse on various sins (lines 197–374 in the present edition) which is inserted into the story soon after its beginning. It will be convenient to consider this discourse on the sins first; we may call it the 'sermon-interlude'. In this sermon-interlude the Pardoner displays once more the virtuosity as a preacher that we have already seen in his Prologue. He begins with a long attack on gluttony, fully illustrated with *exempla* and supported by authorities. At various points in this attack he turns to consider one special subdivision of the larger sin of gluttony, namely drunkenness, and to illustrate its unfortunate effects. By this time, he has got fully into his stride, and though he admits that he has said enough of gluttony, he turns back not to his story but to a second sin, gambling:

> Namoore of this, for it may wel suffise.
> And now that I have spoken of glotonye,
> Now wol I yow deffenden hasardrye. (302–4)

Gambling he treats in the same way as gluttony, though more briefly, and then finally he launches an attack on a third sin, swearing. Then at last he returns to the story he had begun nearly two hundred lines earlier.

A denunciation of sins nearly two hundred lines long, inserted at a point when the story has scarcely begun, might seem in great danger of being tedious. This danger is avoided in the sermon-interlude by the extraordinary virtuosity of technique the Pardoner displays in his preaching. The methods he adopts are astonishingly various. At one moment he is quoting sensational stories of incest and murder from the Bible; at another he is giving details of cooking procedures. Sometimes he will denounce sin from the heights, as if his voice were God's;

sometimes he will speak to his listeners with the utmost familiarity and crack sly or knowing jokes as if he were nudging them in the ribs. Now he speaks bluntly and even coarsely; now he displays abstruse learning and dazzles at least the 'lewed' among the pilgrims with his scraps of theology. Variety is the essence of his art: the listeners are never allowed to rest in a single attitude of mind in case they should become bored and inattentive, and he has something for everyone.

His learning in particular demands some comment. As a preacher would be expected to do, the Pardoner bases his argument on the Bible. He quotes or alludes to a wide variety of Scriptural texts—from Genesis, Proverbs and Ecclesiasticus (part of the Apocrypha in the Authorized Version), and from the Gospels and (most often of all) the epistles of St Paul. But he also quotes from at least one theological work, the *Adversus Jovinianum* of St Jerome; from this he takes the somewhat surprising idea that the eating of the apple was an example of the sin of gluttony. And he borrows also from three moralists, the first-century Stoic Seneca and the medieval Christians Pope Innocent III and John of Salisbury. None of this material is particularly recondite; it does not imply especially deep reading on Chaucer's part, but it does indicate that the sermon-interlude is not simply a flashy tissue of in-accuracies such as a real *quaestor* might have produced. It can be seen to possess a firm moral and theological foundation; and this view of it is supported by the unexpectedly close links that exist between it and *The Parson's Tale*.

The Parson's Tale, as has been mentioned, is also a sermon, and it takes the form of an analysis of the seven deadly sins and of the remedies against them, in which each sin and its various subdivisions are distinguished with minute care. In ideas, and even in wording, the sermon-interlude in *The Pardoner's Tale* often echoes the Parson's sermon very closely. On gambling, to take one example, the Parson begins as follows: 'Now comth hasardrie..., of which comth deceite, false othes, chidinges, and alle ravynes, blaspheminge and reneying of God, and hate of his neighebores, wast of goodes, misspendinge of time, and somtime manslaughtre'. The Pardoner introduces his attack on gambling thus:

> Hasard is verray mooder of lesinges,
> And of deceite, and cursed forsweringes,
> Blaspheme of Crist, manslaughtre, and wast also
> Of catel and of time.... (305–8)

The two passages are clearly similar, though the Pardoner has carefully selected from the Parson's unartistically long list, and, with a revealingly characteristic perversion, has altered the order of the last three items so as to make waste of time and goods sound *more* important than manslaughter. Underlying the attractive variety of the sermon-interlude's surface can be found a theological exactness which may not be 'realistic', but which implies a theologically sensitive poet and audience.

But what is the effect of all the Pardoner's rhetoric and theology? He speaks what purports to be a prohibition of the sins of gluttony, gambling, and swearing—'Now wol I yow *deffenden* [forbid] hasardrye'—and yet the effect of his preaching is not really prohibitive. By it the sins are not diminished but magnified: they come to assume gigantic proportions and a relentless activity which is given them by the vigour of Chaucer's verse and by its constant movement from one *exemplum* to another. They come to seem irresistible forces, at work wherever in time or place one turns one's glance; and, like the Pardoner himself, they arouse at the same time horror and fascination.

This ambivalent reaction is also provoked by another, related aspect of the Pardoner's treatment of the sins. As he presents them, they merge into one another. Gluttony leads to lechery, as the *exemplum* of Lot witnesses; it was also the cause of the fall of man. Gambling leads to the results listed above, including lying, murder, and blasphemy, and also, as a later line insists, to other sins: 'Forswering, ire, falsenesse, homicide'. This last line occurs in the attack on swearing, and thus has the effect of blurring the distinction between that sin and the others. In the furnace of the Pardoner's rhetoric, all the sins are fused together into a mass more powerful and more terrifying than any single sin could be. If that mass could be given a name, it would be blasphemy. Gluttony is a form of blasphemy, as appears from St Paul's 'wombe is hir God' (line 247; compare Epistle to the Philippians iii. 19), applied to gluttons. Gambling, as has been said, leads to 'cursed forsweringes' and 'blaspheme of Crist'. And the sermon-interlude culminates in a twenty-seven-line section devoted to blasphemy itself. In this the Pardoner argues that God forbids taking His name in vain even more urgently than he forbids murder (because the prohibition of blasphemy comes earlier in the list of Commandments). He goes on to give examples of verbal blasphemies such as medieval gamblers might use—'By Goddes precious herte', 'By Goddes armes', and so on. From these examples he passes directly back into the tale of the three revellers.

The process by which the sins are subsumed into a greater whole and culminate in blasphemy is relevant to the actual tale as well as the sermon-interlude. I have called it an interlude, and other readers have gone further and denied that it is at all relevant to the actual story. It has even been suggested that the interlude was originally intended for the Parson, and that the story-opening which precedes was intended to introduce a quite different tale from the one the Pardoner actually goes on to tell.[1] But in fact the interlude is closely connected with the tale of the three revellers. For in them the sins are synthesized as they are in the interlude: they are gluttons, gamblers, time-wasters, deceivers, murderers, and above all blasphemers. (The nature of their blasphemy will be discussed below, but the fact is clear.) It is the interlude which makes it seem natural that the theme *Radix malorum est cupiditas* should be illustrated by a tale about three blasphemous revellers; for all the sins have been fused into blasphemy in the Prologue, and their avarice is only one aspect of their general sinfulness.

The Tale resumed

At last, then, after all this preparation, we come to the resumption of the Tale itself. We have seen that the story was not invented by Chaucer, but borrowed from an extensive tradition. Chaucer's task, here as so often in his work, was to give new life and meaning to an old tale. Some of the meaning he gives it is supplied by the sermon-interlude we have just been looking at; this is his own

[1] Carleton Brown (ed.), *The Pardoner's Tale* (Oxford, 1935), pp. xv–xx.

contribution entirely, and in others of *The Canterbury Tales* too he indicates the area in which we are to look for a story's significance by inserting an apparent digression soon after the story has begun. Other meanings that he finds in the actual narrative of *The Pardoner's Tale* we shall come to in a minute. But the life he gives it, through his skill as a narrative and dramatic poet, is incomparable and unmistakable; here the modern reader is unlikely to need persuasion.

Realistic speech

First, he cannot fail to respond to the realistic speech that Chaucer gives his characters. The existing story supplies the outline, but it is Chaucer who colours it in with speech that conveys tones of voice and shades of human relationship with brilliant directness. No 'stage-directions' are necessary: all is present in the verse itself, which always implies a speaking voice and controls that voice's tone. There is, for example, the speech by the serving boy of one of the revellers, in reply to his master's asking whose corpse is being carried past. He answers with naïve eagerness that the dead man was an old friend of his master's: 'He was, pardee, an old felawe of youres' (386). Boyishly, he is proud that he knows the answer without going to inquire, and so he brings out the unpleasant truth with no tactful evasion. His youth also makes it natural that he should conceive of death literally as it was portrayed symbolically in medieval art: a silent murderer armed with a spear. And, naturally, he relies not on any experiences of his own but on his mother's traditional wisdom—'Thus taughte me my dame'—when he warns his master to make careful preparation before meeting such a powerful adversary. All that he says seems to offer a warning, and it is the more effective because it is delivered with an innocent enthusiasm which implies that he himself fails to recognize its significance.

Realistic speech of a quite different kind is displayed in the brief 'temptation-scene' which takes place between the two remaining revellers when the youngest has been sent to fetch food and drink. The 'worst' of the three has already betrayed his attitude towards the find in a quickly corrected slip of the tongue:

> But mighte this gold be caried fro this place
> Hoom to myn hous—or elles unto youres
> (For wel ye woot that al this gold is oures).... (498–500)

They are accomplices in *cupiditas*, but *cupiditas*, by its very nature, is bound to split up their fellowship. At the first opportunity, one of them—presumably the same one, their constant leading spirit—suggests a plan to his companion. They will kill the third on his return, and so the treasure will be split between two, not three. But he goes about the matter with the utmost circumspection. First, he simply outlines the situation in terms of power and profit: two shares would each be larger than three, and two men together would be stronger than one. Only when his companion is intrigued enough to offer secrecy does he put forward his actual proposal of a cold-blooded murder. His character, which seems the very embodiment of *cupiditas* itself, is beautifully revealed in his attitude towards friendship. The three are friends and sworn brothers, yet it is friendship he invokes in proposing that two of them should murder their friend, and there is a serpentine cunning in his repetitions:'Hadde I nat doon a *freendes* torn

34

to thee?...My deere freend...'. And his actual proposal, when he makes it, again depends on exploiting friendship, and is offered with a casual brutality that is equally revealing and convincing:

> Looke whan that he is set, that right anoon
> Aris as though thou woldest with him pleye,
> And I shal rive him thurgh the sides tweye
> Whil that thou strogelest with him as in game,
> And with thy daggere looke thou do the same. (540–4)

His companion is at first baffled by his oblique approach, and his puzzlement is beautifully conveyed in his questions: 'What shal we doon? What shal we to him seye?'. He is cautious in promising only secrecy, not help; but it is enough. The hook is baited, and he swallows it. The remainder of the dialogue is already implied, and Chaucer, with the marvellous economy that characterizes his telling of the tale, can break the conversation short at the proposal of murder and the vision of desire fulfilled in endless games of *hasard*. We know the essentials, and can fill in the rest for ourselves.

The pace of the story

Life is given to the story in another way by Chaucer's control of its pace. The actual story is strikingly brief—only one-third of the whole text—and its brevity stands out all the more sharply against the expansive material by which it is surrounded. The three revellers, unmentioned previously, are introduced with abrupt familiarity, as if we knew them already:

> Thise riotoures thre of whiche I telle. (375)

The essentials of the opening scene are immediately set before us: the three revellers, already drinking at dawn, unmindful of the canonical hours, and a single sound-effect, the sinister noise of the bell being carried along in front of a corpse on its way to burial. There is no superfluous description, yet the scene is set with brilliant exactness, and the action is under way almost before we are aware of it. In what follows, brief tableaux of discussion alternate with rapid and decisive movements. The servant and the innkeeper speak of Death's power, and, with the mad rashness for which the 'first' reveller is usually spokesman—the rashness that the rapid movement of the narrative expresses—they decide to kill Death, and rush off 'al dronken in this rage' to find him. There is then a pause imposed by the meeting with the deliberately-spoken old man—

> This olde man gan looke in his visage,
> And seyde thus...   (434–5)

—followed by a new surge of activity when he directs them to the oak tree. They run, and the rhythmic emphasis falls on the verb of motion:

> And everich of thise riotoures *ran*
> Til he cam to that tree.   (482–3)

Now comes another pause for discussion. The 'worst' reveller expounds his plan (or the part of it which can be told to the youngest), then the youngest is sent off to the town, and there follows the 'temptation scene'. Simultaneously with this, the youngest has thought of his plan, and he too is jerked into rapid activity. He hurries—'no lenger wolde he tarie'—to the apothecary, and buys a poison which will take effect equally hurriedly:

> Ye, sterve he shal, and that in lasse while
> Than thou wolt goon a paas nat but a mile,
> This poisoun is so strong and violent.   (579–81)

Having obtained the poison, he runs (with 'ran' again emphasized as the rhyme-word) to borrow the bottles and returns to his companions. The closing events of the story—the treacherous murder and the double poisoning—are narrated without delay or artifice. 'What nedeth it to sermone of it moore?', asks the Pardoner; everything happened as planned. The pace of the narrative, at first interrupted by threatening tableaux, but gradually increasing to an almost grotesque violence, as though a film were being gradually speeded up, is expressive of the very nature of the story. It shows a kind of madness in the revellers, as, not satisfied with the inevitable approach of death, they hurl themselves towards their own death (and damnation too). Once, with the *dénouement*, the conclusion of the actual story is reached, the pace immediately slackens, and the Pardoner allows himself to expand on the simple event with a learned allusion to Avicenna and a series of rhetorical apostrophes.

The old man

Another way in which Chaucer gives new life to an old tale is one which derives from the old tale itself. The basic story of the quest for death depends on our understanding the personification of death as literally true, not metaphorical, until it emerges that the revellers 'find Death' not as a person but in the shape of their own *cupiditas*.

> No lenger thanne after Deeth they soughte   (486)

comments the Pardoner when the revellers come upon the

37

heap of gold; they do not need to seek for death any longer, because they have already found it. But Chaucer greatly expands the literalism of the story. He constantly makes his characters treat common metaphors as literal statements, and this gives the work a primitive, mythological quality. Death is a person to the innkeeper and the revellers as well as the boy: he is a 'privee theef', a 'false traitour', a dangerous enemy, who may 'do a man a dishonour', but, being a person, is capable of being killed. There is literalism too in the recurrent idea that the revellers' oaths by the parts of Christ's body are actually tearing that body to pieces. And the literalism of Chaucer's treatment centres in the mysterious old man whom the revellers meet.

The significance of this old man has been the subject of much controversy among Chaucer's readers: he is a figure of compelling power, but it is not obvious what his status is in the poem's scheme of ideas. A common view is that he is himself Death; but surely the fact that he is seeking for death, and that he points out the way to death for the revellers, makes this interpretation unlikely. They are mistaken, after all, in thinking that death is a being external to themselves: death for them lies within them, in the nature of their murderously egoistic desire for possessions.

One scholar sees the old man as an allegorical figure standing for the *vetus homo* of St Paul, the 'old man, which is corrupt according to the deceitful lusts', and which must be cast off before one can assume the 'new man, which after God is created in righteousness and true holiness'.[1] This view, however, involves us in seeing the

---

[1] St Paul, Epistle to the Ephesians iv. 22–4. See R. P. Miller, 'Chaucer's Pardoner, the Scriptural Eunuch and the *Pardoner's Tale*', *Speculum*, XXX (1955), 180–99.

old man as an evil figure; and that is not at all how he is actually presented in the Tale. He retains some of the characteristics of the wise philosopher or hermit in the original folk-tale, and he quotes Scripture to rebuke the revellers for not showing respect to his age. The effect of the Tale is plainly to suggest that their lack of respect for him is one reason for their punishment. Chaucer is unlikely to include an allegorical level of meaning which runs directly counter to the literal sense of his story.

Another commentator asserts that the old man is merely an old man, to be understood solely in realistic terms; when he directs the revellers down the crooked path to the oak tree, he does so at random, not knowing what they will find there, because he is frightened by their threats and wants to get rid of them.[1] Yet the 'croked wey' down which he directs them clearly has symbolic associations with sin, and it would be drawing too fine a distinction to suggest that Chaucer intends us to be aware of this symbolism and at the same time to realize that the old man is not aware of it. And in any case the old man as Chaucer presents him possesses a poetic suggestiveness, a resonance, which this simplifying explanation would exclude.

This resonance is what the old man primarily contributes to the poem, and perhaps the contribution may not be precisely identifiable in intellectual terms. The Tale as a whole centres in a quest for death; this quest is presented in an extended form in the actions of the three revellers, but in a different, more concentrated form it is embodied in the old man. He is seeking death not in order

[1] W. J. B. Owen, 'The Old Man in *The Pardoner's Tale*', *Review of English Studies*, n.s. II (1951), 49–55.

to destroy it but in order to die; and death evades him in a way which contrasts ironically with the way in which it lies in wait for the revellers. In him death and its approach take on a horrifyingly concrete form. If he could find someone to exchange youth for his age, he would wish to go on living; if he could die, he would; but instead he is condemned to a permanent old age. His face is 'ful pale and welked', and he refers to the wasting away of his 'flessh and blood and skin' as if it were a process occurring visibly before the revellers' eyes. By a common metaphor, the earth is our mother, and he treats this metaphor as literally true, and knocks continually on the earth with his stick, saying, 'Leeve mooder, leet me in!'. It is difficult to imagine a more sinister way of describing the constant tap of an old man's stick as he walks about. And he expresses his wish to die in another vividly concrete form, and one which reminds us of the vanity of earthly life: he wishes he could exchange his chestful of clothes for the 'heyre clowt' in which a dead man is wrapped in his coffin. In this figure, on the brink of death, yet not dead, the wretched subjection of human existence to death is conveyed more powerfully than it could be by straightforward theological assertion. The revellers delight in their life in this world, and yet this is what it amounts to: a state of being in which death itself must be begged for. The old man is a figure at once inescapably concrete and disturbingly suggestive: he produces a shiver of apprehension, a physiological response which can never be fully resolved into a statement of 'meaning'.

Blasphemy in the Tale

The old man, then, is used by Chaucer to open a door into a new dimension of his Tale—a door through which blows the cold air of mortality. If Chaucer had not added him to the story of the three revellers, its significance would be greatly lessened. But there is another level of significance in *The Pardoner's Tale* which is implicit in the story itself, and which Chaucer has brought into the open with many small touches. This is perhaps its deepest significance of all. The Pardoner, we have seen, is a blasphemer: his very way of life is a blasphemous parody of the divine values it ought properly to serve. We have also seen how he interrupts his Tale with a homiletic interlude culminating in an attack on blasphemy. The Tale is about blasphemers: not only are the revellers' other sins forms of blasphemy, but they persistently commit verbal assaults on the body of Christ. We are told of these in the first section of the story:

> Hir othes been so grete and so dampnable
> That it is grisly for to heere hem swere.
> Oure blissed Lordes body they totere,—
> Hem thoughte that Jewes rente him noght ynough.
> (186–9)

After the sermon-interlude we hear examples of how the revellers tear Christ's body to pieces, and they are of the same type as those mentioned under blasphemy in the interlude: 'Ye, Goddes armes', 'I make avow to Goddes digne bones', 'By Goddes dignitee'. Oaths such as these echo throughout the Tale, and serve to create an irony by which the revellers come under a divine judgement which they themselves invoke. A particularly striking example of how God's name is thus taken in vain, and yet not in vain, occurs when the youngest reveller is alone, and

> 'O Lord!' quod he, 'if so were that I mighte
> Have al this tresor to myself allone,
> Ther is no man that liveth under the trone
> Of God that sholde live so murye as I.' (554–7)

At that very moment he is before God's throne, the seat of judgement, and does not know it. But the oaths come most thickly earlier in the Tale, when the revellers are making their vow

> To live and dien ech of hem for oother. (417)

They swear 'many a grisly ooth', and we are reminded that in doing so they tear Christ's body to pieces. Here again, once we know the story, we feel the terrifying irony by which God brings men to the ill ends they themselves desire.

The purpose of their vow, however, brings us to another kind of blasphemy: a blasphemous parody of the sacred, embodied in the very shape of the narrative. Their purpose is to bring about the death of Death: 'Deeth shal be deed, if that they may him hente'. But this concept of the death of Death, *mors mortis*, is a formulation traditionally used by Christian writers to express Christ's victory in the Crucifixion. It goes back to an Old Testament source, Hosea xiii. 14: *O mors, ero mors tua*, 'O death, I will be thy death'.[1] The Latin text is quoted as a prophecy of the triumph of the cross in a number of medieval literary works—Langland's *Piers Plowman* for example. Thus the revellers' purpose is presented as a

---

[1] This is the Douai translation of the Vulgate Bible; the Authorized Version has a different reading.

profane parody of God's purpose in the Crucifixion. In this way, the Tale is exquisitely suitable for the Pardoner to tell; nor need it surprise us that Chaucer should have thought of giving him a story which parodies something holy.

Blasphemous parody was a not uncommon element even in the religious literature of the Middle Ages. In a time when Christianity was unquestioned, blasphemy was perhaps more shocking than it is today, but it was also more possible (because the structure of Christianity stood too firm to be fundamentally shaken by it) and more likely (as the human reaction against an overwhelming current of reverence). In medieval religious drama, Antichrist sometimes appeared as a parody of Christ; and, even more striking, in the *Second Shepherds' Play* of the Towneley cycle—a nativity play—the Lamb of God appears in a comic parody as a stolen sheep hidden in a cradle and disguised as the newborn child of the thief's wife. There, blasphemy co-exists with reverence and is eventually absorbed into a reverence which is the more moving and more secure against irony for including it. In *The Pardoner's Tale*, the blasphemy penetrates to the very structure of the story itself, as it has penetrated to the core of the Pardoner's being; and the teller and his Tale testify to the truth by reversing it, as a photographic negative 'parodies' the positive.

In the Tale, blasphemy appears elsewhere than in the quest to kill Death. The death of Death, in the sacred sense, is brought about by the sacrificial death of Christ on the Cross. However, as a result of the doctrine of the Trinity, this death can easily be represented not as a voluntary self-sacrifice by the Son, but as the sacrifice of a purely passive Son by the other members of the Trinity. Only a small shift of emphasis in this view would create a theory of the Crucifixion as a conspiracy by two members of the Trinity against the third. It appears that in the fourteenth century this shift of emphasis had occurred, and the conspiracy-theory of the Crucifixion had become a current blasphemy. It is mentioned in *Piers Plowman* in a passage regretting that those who can tell of sacred matters are not welcome at feasts. On the contrary, indeed,

> Now is the manere atte mete, when mynstralles ben stylle,
> The lewede ayens the lered the holy lore to dispute,
> And tellen of the Trinite how two slowe the thridde.[1]

> It is now the custom at meal-times, when the minstrels are silent, for the ignorant to argue with the learned about sacred doctrine; and, concerning the Trinity, they say that two killed the third.

If this was a familar idea among the *lewede* (ignorant) in the late fourteenth century, it seems plausible to suppose that the audience of *The Pardoner's Tale*, alerted to blasphemous parody by the 'death of Death' motif, might find a similar parody in the part of the story in which two of a trio of revellers plot to kill the third. The third who is sent away and then murdered thus becomes a parody-representation of Christ. When he returns, the others 'rive him thurgh the sides tweye', tearing his body as Christ's body was torn on the Cross and as it is torn again by the revellers' oaths. The blasphemous meaning is underlined by the fact that the provisions the youngest reveller is sent to fetch are specified as 'breed and wyn'— the two components of the sacrament provided by Christ's

---

[1] *The Vision of William Concerning Piers the Plowman*, ed. W. W. Skeat (rev. ed., Oxford, 1954), C, XII, 35–7.

torn body. Though the story of the three revellers derives from a folk-tale, Chaucer, by adding *The Pardoner's Prologue* and the sermon-interlude, has given it a sufficiently theological treatment for us to gather that his audience had some sensitivity to theological issues. Not a very high degree of theological sensitivity would be needed for the interlocking narrative blasphemies of the Tale to become evident. They provide a significance of the most appropriate kind.

THE CONCLUSION

The end of the story of the three revellers comes with their death, and this event is described by the Pardoner with a bareness, almost an offhandedness, which implies that it is the most natural thing in the world. There is, we may suppose, the briefest of pauses, while the pilgrims take in the significance of what has been narrated so rapidly. And then, immediately, the Pardoner resumes the expansive and even inflated style that he had used in his sermon-interlude. First, he refers us to a scientific authority, the great Arab physician Avicenna, for an account of the 'signes of empoisoning' displayed on the corpses of the two elder revellers—as if, for these materially minded evildoers, the damnation of the soul were represented in the distortion of the body. Then he suddenly lets fly with a thunder of *exclamationes* directed against the sins of the murderers, and reaching a climax, as usual, in blasphemy. Then, equally suddenly, the 'O' of denunciation gives way to the 'Allas' of pleading, and he asks tearfully how mankind can behave so unnaturally towards its Creator and Redeemer. With another unexpected switch, he turns from warning 'mankinde' against the sins to warning the 'goode men' who are listening to him against the 'sinne of avarice'—the whole purpose of his preaching. In persuasively jaunty rhythms he invites his congregation to make their offerings on the spot, and assures them that they will swiftly be translated from names on his list to happy souls in 'the blisse of hevene'—the very note of the insurance-salesman. Then, without warning, we are brought back to earth half-way through a line with 'And lo, sires, thus I preche'. It is not us or the pilgrims he is addressing, after all, but an imaginary congregation of the ignorant; we remember that his whole Tale has been only a sample of his preaching skill. If, as is likely, we have forgotten this in the excitement of the narrative, we shall be taken aback for the moment, and, while we are still reeling, the Pardoner comes up with something even more surprising:

> And lo, sires, thus I preche.
> And Jhesu Crist, that is oure soules leche,
> So graunte yow his pardoun to receive,
> For that is best; I wol yow nat deceive. (629–32)

The Pardoner seems to be saying that, though he may deceive his usual audiences, he will not deceive the pilgrims: to them he will admit that Christ's pardon alone, and not his, has power to heal the soul. Some readers have detected in these words a depth of personal feeling that is not to be found in the rest of his patter; as though he felt a momentary repulsion against all his blasphemous falsehood—'a very paroxysm of agonized sincerity', as one scholar has put it[1]—and offered the pilgrims a last desperate glimpse of the truth against which he had

[1] Kittredge, *Chaucer and his Poetry*, p. 217.

blasphemed. What he says *is* the truth, of course, and in distinguishing sharply between Christ's pardon and the 'pardon' a *quaestor* offers he is stating a commonplace of medieval religious literature. But to assert that, in telling the truth, he is 'sincere' is another matter. The devil can quote Scripture to his purpose; and this 'sincerity' seems to be only part of a confidence-trick. With yet another unexpected change of direction, the Pardoner continues:

> But sires, o word forgat I in my tale:
> I have relikes and pardoun in my male
> As faire as any man in Engelond,
> Whiche were me yeven by the popes hond.
> If any of yow wole, of devocion,
> Offren, and han myn absolucion,
> Com forth anon, and kneleth heere adoun,
> And mekely receiveth my pardoun.   (633–40)

He has the impudence to try the technique he has just been demonstrating on the pilgrims themselves—evidently in the hope that, while they are still under the spell of his Tale, he will have the double satisfaction of first showing them how clever he is as a swindler and then swindling them too. Perhaps it is not enough, though, to claim that he is simply insincere in his words about Christ's pardon. That may be as misleading as to claim that he is sincere. His whole method as a preacher is that of self-dramatization: he exploits his own ready emotions by making them public for the sake of gain. By working himself up he works up his audience. No doubt there are real tears in his eyes, but to speak of sincerity or insincerity is as meaningless as it would be if applied to a great actor in a play. He is neither sincere nor insincere; he is simply acting, squeezing the utmost emotion out of his own

47

situation. His wickedness lies in having turned his own moral and spiritual life, and Christian truth itself, into a play.

The Pardoner continues to direct his jaunty patter at the pilgrims. He tempts them with the thought of pardon 'al newe and fressh', like hot cakes. He reminds them, with some relish, that one or two of them may fall from their horses and break their necks on that very journey. Finally, tempting providence, he suggests that the Host himself should set the example in making an offering and kissing the relics, 'For he is moost envoluped in sinne'. Will the Host be able to find a response adequate to this supreme audacity? He does not disappoint us. Like a Dr Johnson of the medieval alehouse, he sweeps the Pardoner away, utterly annihilates him, with a superb explosion of coarseness, devoted mainly to the Pardoner's lack of sexual capacity. It does its work so effectively that the Pardoner is reduced to silence—he who made such a good living by his tongue, and who managed to interrupt even the incessantly loquacious Wife of Bath. The Host seems scarcely aware of his own power in invective: he is puzzled and hurt at the Pardoner's failure to reply, and says he will not play with anyone so quick to lose his temper. Everyone laughs; but the Knight, always tactful, and conscious of his responsibilities as the pilgrim of highest social rank, speaks politely to both, and persuades them to kiss and make up. With that unlikely embrace the Tale ends and the pilgrims ride on.

In the conclusion of *The Pardoner's Tale* Chaucer has displayed one of his most characteristic gifts with supreme virtuosity. He is always the poet of variety, of varying attitudes towards life and varying tones of voice; not, like Milton or Wordsworth, of a single view of the world and a single gravity of utterance. Some of his finest work is in what might be called the poetry of transitions: movements from one fictional world to another, with an utterly different atmosphere. In this conclusion, we are led from the sinister world of the actual story back to the cheerful harmony of the pilgrimage that frames it through a daring series of modulations of feeling. Each shift is surprising, and causes a reassessment of what has preceded; yet each is convincing and unmistakably solid in itself. With each shift we are moved further away from the absorbing horrors of the story, and it takes its place eventually as only one view of a life which can finally be contemplated with sane good humour.

NOTE ON THE TEXT

The text which follows is based upon that of F. N. Robinson (*The Complete Works of Geoffrey Chaucer*, 2nd ed., 1957). The punctuation has been revised, with special reference to the exclamation marks. Spelling has been partly rationalized, by substituting *i* for *y* wherever the change aids the modern reader and does not affect the semantic value of the word. Thus *smylyng* becomes 'smiling', and *nyghtyngale* 'nightingale', but *wyn* (wine), *lyk* (like), and *fyr* (fire) are allowed to stand.

No accentuation has been provided in this text, for two reasons. First, because it produces a page displeasing to the eye; secondly, because it no longer seems necessary or entirely reliable in the light of modern scholarship. It is not now thought that the later works of Chaucer were written in a ten-syllable line from which no variation was permissible. The correct reading of a line of Chaucer is now seen to be more closely related to the correct reading of a comparable line of prose with phrasing suited to the rhythms of speech. This allows the reader to be more flexible in his interpretation of the line, and makes it unreasonably pedantic to provide a rigid system of accentuation.

NOTE ON PRONUNCIATION

These equivalences are intended to offer only a rough guide. For further detail, see *An Introduction to Chaucer*.

SHORT VOWELS

ă represents the sound now written *u*, as in 'cut'
ĕ as in modern 'set'
ĭ as in modern 'is'
ŏ as in modern 'top'
ŭ as in modern 'put' (not as in 'cut')
final -*e* represents the neutral vowel sound in '*a*bout' or 'attent*io*n'. It is silent when the next word in the line begins with a vowel or an *h*.

Note on the Text

LONG VOWELS

ā as in modern 'car' (not as in 'name')

ē (open—i.e. where the equivalent modern word is spelt with *ea*) as in modern 'there'

ē (close—i.e. where the equivalent modern word is spelt with *ee* or *e*) represents the sound now written *a* as in 'take'

ī as in modern 'machine' (not as in 'like')

ō (open—i.e. where the equivalent modern vowel is pronounced as in 'br*o*ther', 'm*oo*d', or 'g*oo*d') represents the sound now written *aw* as in 'fawn'

ō (close—i.e. where the equivalent modern vowel is pronounced as in 'road') as in modern 'note'

ū as in French *tu* or German *Tür*

DIPHTHONGS

ai and *ei* both roughly represent the sound now written *i* or *y* as in 'die' or 'dye'

au and *aw* both represent the sound now written *ow* or *ou* as in 'now' or 'pounce'

ou and *ow* have two pronunciations: as in *through* where the equivalent modern vowel is pronounced as in 'through' or 'mouse'; and as in *pounce* where the equivalent modern vowel is pronounced as in 'know' or 'thought'

WRITING OF VOWELS AND DIPHTHONGS

A long vowel is often indicated by doubling, as in *roote* or *eek*. The *ŭ* sound is sometimes represented by an *o* as in *yong*. The *au* sound is sometimes represented by an *a*, especially before *m* or *n*, as in *cha(u)mbre* or *cha(u)nce*.

CONSONANTS

Largely as in modern English, except that many consonants now silent were still pronounced. *Gh* was pronounced as in Scottish 'lo*ch*', and both consonants should be pronounced in such groups as the following: '*gn*acchen', '*kn*ave', 'wor*d*', 'fol*k*', '*w*rong'.

THE INTRODUCTION TO
THE PARDONER'S TALE

Oure Hooste gan to swere as he were wood;
'Harrow!' quod he, 'by nailes and by blood!
This was a fals cherl and a fals justise.
As shameful deeth as herte may devise
Come to thise juges and hire advocats!
Algate this sely maide is slain, allas!
Allas, to deere boughte she beautee!
Wherfore I seye al day that men may see
That yiftes of Fortune and of Nature
Been cause of deeth to many a creature.   10
Hire beautee was hire deth, I dar wel sayn.
Allas, so pitously as she was slain!
Of bothe yiftes that I speke of now
Men han ful ofte moore for harm than prow.
But trewely, myn owene maister deere,
This is a pitous tale for to heere.
But nathelees, passe over, is no fors.
I pray to God so save thy gentil cors,
And eek thine urinals and thy jurdones,
Thyn ypocras, and eek thy galiones,   20
And every boyste ful of thy letuarie;
God blesse hem, and oure lady Seinte Marie.
So moot I theen, thou art a propre man,
And lyk a prelat, by Seint Ronyan!
Seyde I nat wel? I kan nat speke in terme;
But wel I woot thou doost myn herte to erme,
That I almoost have caught a cardynacle.

53

By Corpus bones! but I have triacle,
Or elles a draughte of moiste and corny ale,
Or but I heere anon a myrie tale,
Myn herte is lost for pitee of this maide.
Thou beel ami, thou Pardoner,' he saide,
'Telle us som mirthe or japes right anon.'

'It shal be doon,' quod he, 'by Seint Ronyon!
But first,' quod he, 'heere at this alestake
I wol bothe drinke, and eten of a cake.'

But right anon thise gentils gonne to crye,
'Nay, lat him telle us of no ribaudye!
Telle us som moral thing, that we may leere
Som wit, and thanne wol we gladly heere.'

'I graunte, ywis,' quod he, 'but I moot thinke
Upon som honest thing while that I drinke.'

THE PARDONER'S PROLOGUE

'Lordinges,' quod he, 'in chirches whan I preche,
I peyne me to han an hauteyn speche,
And ringe it out as round as gooth a belle,
For I kan al by rote that I telle.
My theme is alwey oon, and evere was—
Radix malorum est Cupiditas.
    First I pronounce whennes that I come,
And thanne my bulles shewe I, alle and some.   50
Oure lige lordes seel on my patente,
That shewe I first, my body to warente,
That no man be so boold, ne preest ne clerk,
Me to destourbe of Cristes hooly werk.
And after that thanne telle I forth my tales.
Bulles of popes and of cardinales,
Of patriarkes and bishopes I shewe,
And in Latin I speke a wordes fewe,
To saffron with my predicacioun,
And for to stire hem to devocioun.   60
Thanne shewe I forth my longe cristal stones,
Ycrammed ful of cloutes and of bones,—
Relikes been they, as wenen they echoon.
Thanne have I in latoun a sholder-boon
Which that was of an hooly Jewes sheep.
"Goode men," I seye, "taak of my wordes keep;
If that this boon be wasshe in any welle,
If cow, or calf, or sheep, or oxe swelle
That any worm hath ete, or worm ystonge,
Taak water of that welle and wassh his tonge,   70
And it is hool anon; and forthermoore,

Of pokkes and of scabbe and every soore
Shal every sheep be hool that of this welle
Drinketh a draughte. Taak kep eek what I telle:
If that the good-man that the beestes oweth
Wol every wyke, er that the cok him croweth,
Fastinge, drinken of this welle a draughte,
As thilke hooly Jew oure eldres taughte,
His beestes and his stoor shal multiplie.

80   And, sires, also it heeleth jalousie;
For though a man be falle in jalous rage,
Lat maken with this water his potage,
And nevere shal he moore his wif mistriste,
Though he the soothe of hir defaute wiste,
Al had she taken prestes two or thre.

Heere is a miteyn eek, that ye may se.
He that his hand wol putte in this mitayn,
He shal have multiplying of his grain,
Whan he hath sowen, be it whete or otes,
90   So that he offre pens, or elles grotes.

Goode men and wommen, o thing warne I yow:
If any wight be in this chirche now
That hath doon sinne horrible, that he
Dar nat for shame of it yshriven be,
Or any womman, be she yong or old,
That hath ymaad hir housbonde cokewold,
Swich folk shal have no power ne no grace
To offren to my relikes in this place.
And whoso findeth him out of swich blame,
100   He wol come up and offre in Goddes name,
And I assoille him by the auctoritee
Which that by bulle ygraunted was to me."

By this gaude have I wonne, yeer by yeer,

An hundred mark sith I was pardoner.
I stonde lyk a clerk in my pulpet,
And whan the lewed peple is doun yset,
I preche so as ye han herd bifoore,
And telle an hundred false japes moore.
Thanne peyne I me to strecche forth the nekke,
And est and west upon the peple I bekke,   110
As dooth a dowve sittinge on a berne.
Mine handes and my tonge goon so yerne
That it is joye to se my bisynesse.
Of avarice and of swich cursednesse
Is al my preching, for to make hem free
To yeven hir pens, and namely unto me.
For myn entente is nat but for to winne,
And nothing for correccioun of sinne.
I rekke nevere, whan that they been beried,
Though that hir soules goon a-blakeberied.   120
For certes, many a predicacioun
Comth ofte time of yvel entencioun;
Som for plesance of folk and flaterye,
To been avaunced by ypocrisye,
And som for veyne glorie, and som for hate.
For whan I dar noon oother weyes debate,
Thanne wol I stinge him with my tonge smerte
In preching, so that he shal nat asterte
To been defamed falsly, if that he
Hath trespased to my bretheren or to me.   130
For though I telle noght his propre name,
Men shal wel knowe that it is the same
By signes, and by othere circumstances.
Thus quyte I folk that doon us displesances;
Thus spitte I out my venym under hewe

Of hoolinesse, to semen hooly and trewe.
    But shortly myn entente I wol devise:
I preche of no thing but for coveitise.
Therfore my theme is yet, and evere was,
Radix malorum est Cupiditas.
Thus kan I preche again that same vice
Which that I use, and that is avarice.
But though myself be gilty in that sinne,
Yet kan I maken oother folk to twynne
From avarice, and soore to repente.
But that is nat my principal entente;
I preche nothing but for coveitise.
Of this mateere it oghte ynogh suffise.
    Thanne telle I hem ensamples many oon
Of olde stories longe time agoon.
For lewed peple loven tales olde;
Swiche thinges kan they wel reporte and holde.
What, trowe ye that whiles I may preche,
And winne gold and silver for I teche,
That I wol live in poverte wilfully?
Nay, nay, I thoghte it nevere, trewely!
For I wol preche and begge in sondry landes;
I wol nat do no labour with mine handes,
Ne make baskettes, and live therby,
By cause I wol nat beggen idelly.
I wol noon of the apostles countrefete;
I wol have moneie, wolle, chese, and whete,
Al were it yeven of the povereste page,
Or of the povereste widwe in a village,
Al sholde hir children sterve for famine.
Nay, I wol drinke licour of the vine,
And have a joly wenche in every toun.

140
150
160

But herkneth, lordinges, in conclusioun:
Youre liking is that I shal telle a tale.
Now have I dronke a draughte of corny ale,　　　170
By God, I hope I shal yow telle a thing
That shal by reson been at youre liking.
For though myself be a ful vicious man,
A moral tale yet I yow telle kan,
Which I am wont to preche for to winne.
Now hoold youre pees! my tale I wol biginne.'

THE PARDONER'S TALE

In Flaundres whilom was a compaignye
Of yonge folk that haunteden folye,
As riot, hasard, stywes, and tavernes,
Where as with harpes, lutes, and giternes,   180
They daunce and pleyen at dees bothe day and night,
And eten also and drinken over hir might,
Thurgh which they doon the devel sacrifise
Withinne that develes temple, in cursed wise,
By superfluitee abhominable.
Hir othes been so grete and so dampnable
That it is grisly for to heere hem swere.
Oure blissed Lordes body they totere—
Hem thoughte that Jewes rente him noght ynough;
And ech of hem at otheres sinne lough.   190
And right anon thanne comen tombesteres
Fetys and smale, and yonge frutesteres,
Singeres with harpes, baudes, wafereres,
Whiche been the verray develes officeres
To kindle and blowe the fyr of lecherye,
That is annexed unto glotonye.
The hooly writ take I to my witnesse
That luxurie is in wyn and dronkenesse.

Lo, how that dronken Looth, unkindely,
Lay by his doghtres two, unwityngly;   200
So dronke he was, he nyste what he wroghte.

Herodes, whoso wel the stories soghte,
Whan he of wyn was repleet at his feeste,
Right at his owene table he yaf his heeste
To sleen the Baptist John, ful giltelees.

Senec seith a good word doutelees;
He seith he kan no difference finde
Bitwix a man that is out of his minde
And a man which that is dronkelewe,
210   But that woodnesse, yfallen in a shrewe,
Persevereth lenger than doth dronkenesse.
O glotonye, ful of cursednesse!
O cause first of oure confusioun!
O original of oure dampnacioun,
Til Crist hadde boght us with his blood again!
Lo, how deere, shortly for to sayn,
Aboght was thilke cursed vileynye—
Corrupt was al this world for glotonye.

Adam oure fader, and his wyf also,
220   Fro Paradis to labour and to wo
Were driven for that vice, it is no drede.
For whil that Adam fasted, as I rede,
He was in Paradis; and whan that he
Eet of the fruit deffended on the tree,
Anon he was out cast to wo and peyne.
O glotonye, on thee wel oghte us pleyne!
O, wiste a man how manye maladies
Folwen of excesse and of glotonies,
He wolde been the moore mesurable
230   Of his diete, sittinge at his table.
Allas, the shorte throte, the tendre mouth,
Maketh that est and west and north and south,
In erthe, in eir, in water, men to swinke
To gete a glotoun deyntee mete and drinke.
Of this matiere, o Paul, wel kanstow trete:
'Mete unto wombe, and wombe eek unto mete,
Shal God destroyen bothe,' as Paulus seith.

Allas, a foul thing is it, by my feith,
To seye this word, and fouler is the dede,
Whan man so drinketh of the white and rede   240
That of his throte he maketh his privee,
Thurgh thilke cursed superfluitee.
    The apostel weping seith ful pitously,
'Ther walken manye of whiche yow toold have I—
I seye it now weping, with pitous vois—
That they been enemys of Cristes crois,
Of whiche the ende is deeth, wombe is hir god.'
O wombe! O bely! O stinking cod,
Fulfilled of dong and of corrupcioun!
At either ende of thee foul is the soun.   250
How greet labour and cost is thee to finde!
Thise cookes, how they stampe, and streyne, and
        grinde,
And turnen substaunce into accident,
To fulfille al thy likerous talent!
Out of the harde bones knokke they
The mary, for they caste noght awey
That may go thurgh the golet softe and swoote.
Of spicerie of leef and bark and roote
Shal been his sauce ymaked by delit,
To make him yet a newer appetit.   260
But certes, he that haunteth swiche delices
Is deed, whil that he liveth in tho vices.
    A lecherous thing is wyn, and dronkenesse
Is ful of striving and of wrecchednesse.
O dronke man, disfigured is thy face,
Sour is thy breeth, foul artow to embrace,
And thurgh thy dronke nose semeth the soun
As though thou seydest ay 'Sampsoun, Sampsoun!'

And yet, God woot, Sampsoun drank nevere no wyn.
270   Thou fallest as it were a stiked swyn;
Thy tonge is lost, and al thyn honeste cure;
For dronkenesse is verray sepulture
Of mannes wit and his discrecioun.
In whom that drinke hath dominacioun
He kan no conseil kepe, it is no drede.
Now kepe yow fro the white and fro the rede,
And namely fro the white wyn of Lepe,
That is to selle in Fisshstrete or in Chepe.
This wyn of Spaigne crepeth subtilly
280   In othere wines, growinge faste by,
Of which ther riseth swich fumositee
That whan a man hath dronken draughtes thre,
And weneth that he be at hoom in Chepe,
He is in Spaigne, right at the toune of Lepe—
Nat at the Rochele, ne at Burdeux toun;
And thanne wol he seye 'Sampsoun, Sampsoun!'
     But herkneth, lordinges, o word, I yow preye,
That alle the soverein actes, dar I seye,
Of victories in the Olde Testament,
290   Thurgh verray God, that is omnipotent,
Were doon in abstinence and in preyere.
Looketh the Bible, and ther ye may it leere.
     Looke, Attilla, the grete conquerour,
Deyde in his sleep with shame and dishonour,
Bledinge ay at his nose in dronkenesse.
A capitain sholde live in sobrenesse.
And over al this, aviseth yow right wel
What was comaunded unto Lamuel—
Nat Samuel, but Lamuel, seye I;
300   Redeth the Bible, and finde it expresly

Of wyn-yeving to hem that han justise.
Namoore of this, for it may wel suffise.
   And now that I have spoken of glotonye,
Now wol I yow deffenden hasardrye.
Hasard is verray mooder of lesinges,
And of deceite, and cursed forsweringes,
Blaspheme of Crist, manslaughtre, and wast also
Of catel and of time; and forthermo,
It is repreeve and contrarie of honour
For to ben holde a commune hasardour.   310
And ever the hyer he is of estaat,
The moore is he yholden desolaat.
If that a prince useth hasardrye,
In alle governaunce and policye
He is, as by commune opinioun,
Yholde the lasse in reputacioun.
   Stilboun, that was a wys embassadour,
Was sent to Corinthe, in ful greet honour,
Fro Lacidomye, to make hire alliaunce.
And whan he cam, him happede, par chaunce,   320
That alle the gretteste that were of that lond,
Pleyinge atte hasard he hem fond.
For which, as soone as it mighte be,
He stal him hoom again to his contree,
And seyde, 'Ther wol I nat lese my name,
Ne I wol nat take on me so greet defame,
Yow for to allie unto none hasardours.
Sendeth othere wise embassadours;
For, by my trouthe, me were levere die
Than I yow sholde to hasardours allye.   330
For ye, that been so glorious in honours,
Shul nat allyen yow with hasardours

As by my wil, ne as by my tretee.'
This wise philosophre, thus seyde hee.
    Looke eek that to the king Demetrius,
The king of Parthes, as the book seith us,
Sente him a paire of dees of gold in scorn,
For he hadde used hasard ther-biforn;
For which he heeld his glorie or his renoun
340 At no value or reputacioun.
Lordes may finden oother maner pley
Honest ynough to drive the day awey.
    Now wol I speke of othes false and grete
A word or two, as olde bookes trete.
Gret swering is a thing abhominable,
And fals swering is yet moore reprevable.
The heighe God forbad swering at al,
Witnesse on Mathew; but in special
Of swering seith the hooly Jeremye,
350 'Thou shalt swere sooth thine othes, and nat lie,
And swere in doom, and eek in rightwisnesse';
But idel swering is a cursednesse.
Bihoold and se that in the firste table
Of heighe Goddes heestes honurable,
Hou that the seconde heeste of him is this:
'Take nat my name in idel or amis.'
Lo, rather he forbedeth swich swering
Than homicide or many a cursed thing;
I seye that, as by ordre, thus it stondeth;
360 This knoweth, that his heestes understondeth,
How that the seconde heeste of God is that.
And forther over, I wol thee telle al plat,
That vengeance shal nat parten from his hous
That of his othes is to outrageous.

'By Goddes precious herte,' and 'By his nailes,'
And 'By the blood of Crist that is in Hayles,
Sevene is my chaunce, and thyn is cynk and treye!
'By Goddes armes, if thou falsly pleye,
This daggere shal thurghout thyn herte go!'—
This fruit cometh of the bicched bones two,   370
Forswering, ire, falsnesse, homicide.
Now, for the love of Crist, that for us dyde,
Lete youre othes, bothe grete and smale.
But, sires, now wol I telle forth my tale.

   Thise riotoures thre of whiche I telle,
Longe erst er prime rong of any belle,
Were set hem in a taverne for to drinke,
And as they sat, they herde a belle clinke
Biforn a cors, was caried to his grave.
That oon of hem gan callen to his knave: 380
'Go bet,' quod he, 'and axe redily
What cors is this that passeth heer forby;
And looke that thou reporte his name weel.'

   'Sire,' quod this boy, 'it nedeth never-a-deel;
It was me toold er ye cam heer two houres.
He was, pardee, an old felawe of youres;
And sodeynly he was yslain to-night,
Fordronke, as he sat on his bench upright.
Ther cam a privee theef men clepeth Deeth,
That in this contree al the peple sleeth,   390
And with his spere he smoot his herte atwo,
And wente his wey withouten wordes mo.
He hath a thousand slain this pestilence.
And, maister, er ye come in his presence,
Me thinketh that it were necessarie
For to be war of swich an adversarie.

Beth redy for to meete him everemoore;
Thus taughte me my dame; I sey namoore.'
'By seinte Marie,' seyde this taverner,
'The child seith sooth, for he hath slain this yeer,
Henne over a mile, withinne a greet village,
Bothe man and womman, child, and hine, and page;
I trowe his habitacioun be there.
To been avised greet wisdom it were,
Er that he dide a man a dishonour.'

    'Ye, Goddes armes!' quod this riotour,
'Is it swich peril with him for to meete?
I shal him seke by wey and eek by strete,
I make avow to Goddes digne bones!
Herkneth, felawes, we thre been al ones;
Lat ech of us holde up his hand til oother,
And ech of us bicomen otheres brother,
And we wol sleen this false traitour Deeth.
He shal be slain, he that so manye sleeth,
By Goddes dignitee, er it be night.'

    Togidres han thise thre hir trouthes plight
To live and dien ech of hem for oother,
As though he were his owene ybore brother.
And up they stirte, al dronken in this rage,
And forth they goon towardes that village
Of which the taverner hadde spoke biforn.
And many a grisly ooth thanne han they sworn,
And Cristes blessed body al torente—
Deeth shal be deed, if that they may him hente.

    Whan they han goon nat fully half a mile,
Right as they wolde han troden over a stile,
An oold man and a povre with hem mette.
This olde man ful mekely hem grette,

And seyde thus, 'Now, lordes, God yow see!'
   The proudeste of thise riotoures three   430
Answerde again, 'What, carl, with sory grace!
Why artow al forwrapped save thy face?
Why livestow so longe in so greet age?'
   This olde man gan looke in his visage,
And seyde thus: 'For I ne kan nat finde
A man, though that I walked into Inde,
Neither in citee ne in no village,
That wolde chaunge his youthe for myn age;
And therfore moot I han myn age stille,
As longe time as it is Goddes wille.   440
Ne Deeth, allas, ne wol nat han my lyf.
Thus walke I, lyk a restelees kaitif,
And on the ground, which is my moodres gate,
I knokke with my staf, bothe erly and late,
And seye "Leeve mooder, leet me in!
Lo how I vanisshe, flessh and blood and skin!
Allas! whan shul my bones been at reste?
Mooder, with yow wolde I chaunge my cheste
That in my chambre longe time hath be,
Ye, for an heyre clowt to wrappe in me."   450
But yet to me she wol nat do that grace,
For which ful pale and welked is my face.
   But sires, to yow it is no curteisye
To speken to an old man vileynye,
But he trespasse in word, or elles in dede.
In Hooly Writ ye may yourself wel rede:
"Agains an oold man, hoor upon his heed,
Ye sholde arise;" wherfore I yeve yow reed,
Ne dooth unto an oold man noon harm now,
Namoore than that ye wolde men did to yow   460

In age, if that ye so longe abide.
And God be with yow, where ye go or ride!
I moot go thider as I have to go.'
  'Nay, olde cherl, by God, thou shalt nat so,'
Seyde this oother hasardour anon;
'Thou partest nat so lightly, by Seint John!
Thou spak right now of thilke traitour Deeth,
That in this contree alle oure freendes sleeth.
Have heer my trouthe, as thou art his espye,
Telle where he is, or thou shalt it abye,
By God, and by the hooly sacrement!
For soothly thou art oon of his assent
To sleen us yonge folk, thou false theef!'
  'Now, sires,' quod he, 'if that yow be so leef
To finde Deeth, turne up this croked wey,
For in that grove I lafte him, by my fey,
Under a tree, and there he wole abide;
Noght for youre boost he wole him no thing hide.
Se ye that ook? Right there ye shal him finde.
God save yow, that boghte again mankinde,
And yow amende.' Thus seyde this olde man;
And everich of thise riotoures ran
Til he cam to that tree, and ther they founde
Of florins fine of gold ycoined rounde
Wel ny an eighte busshels, as hem thoughte.
No lenger thanne after Deeth they soughte,
But ech of hem so glad was of that sighte,
For that the florins been so faire and brighte,
That doun they sette hem by this precious hoord.
The worste of hem, he spak the firste word.
  'Bretheren,' quod he, 'taak kep what that I seye;
My wit is greet, though that I bourde and pleye.

This tresor hath Fortune unto us yiven,
In mirthe and joliftee oure lyf to liven,
And lightly as it comth, so wol we spende.
Ey! Goddes precious dignitee! who wende
To-day that we sholde han so fair a grace?
But mighte this gold be caried fro this place
Hoom to myn hous—or elles unto youres
(For wel ye woot that al this gold is oures)—   500
Thanne were we in heigh felicitee.
But trewely, by daye it may nat bee.
Men wolde seyn that we were theves stronge,
And for oure owene tresor doon us honge.
This tresor moste ycaried be by nighte
As wisely and as slyly as it mighte.
Wherfore I rede that cut among us alle
Be drawe, and lat se wher the cut wol falle;
And he that hath the cut with herte blithe
Shal renne to the town, and that ful swithe,   510
And bringe us breed and wyn ful prively.
And two of us shul kepen subtilly
This tresor wel; and if he wol nat tarie,
Whan it is night, we wol this tresor carie,
By oon assent, where as us thinketh best.'
That oon of hem the cut broghte in his fest,
And bad hem drawe, and looke where it wol falle;
And it fil on the yongeste of hem alle,
And forth toward the toun he wente anon.
And also soone as that he was gon,   520
That oon of hem spak thus unto that oother:
'Thow knowest wel thou art my sworen brother;
Thy profit wol I telle thee anon.
Thou woost wel that oure felawe is agon.

And heere is gold, and that ful greet plentee,
That shal departed been among us thre.
But nathelees, if I kan shape it so
That it departed were among us two,
Hadde I nat doon a freendes torn to thee?'

530   That oother answerde, 'I noot how that may be.
He woot wel that the gold is with us tweye;
What shal we doon? What shal we to him seye?'
    'Shal it be conseil?' seyde the firste shrewe,
'And I shal tellen in a wordes fewe
What we shal doon, and bringe it wel aboute.'
    'I graunte,' quod that oother, 'out of doute,
That, by my trouthe, I wol thee nat biwreye.'
    'Now,' quod the firste, 'thou woost wel we be tweye,
And two of us shul strenger be than oon.

540   Looke whan that he is set, that right anoon
Aris as though thou woldest with him pleye,
And I shal rive him thurgh the sides tweye
Whil that thou strogelest with him as in game,
And with thy daggere looke thou do the same;
And thanne shal al this gold departed be,
My deere freend, bitwixen me and thee.
Thanne may we bothe oure lustes all fulfille,
And pleye at dees right at oure owene wille.'
And thus acorded been thise shrewes tweye

550   To sleen the thridde, as ye han herd me seye.
    This yongeste, which that wente to the toun,
Ful ofte in herte he rolleth up and doun
The beautee of thise florins newe and brighte.
'O Lord!' quod he, 'if so were that I mighte
Have al this tresor to myself allone,
Ther is no man that liveth under the trone

Of God that sholde live so murye as I.'
And atte laste the feend, oure enemy,
Putte in his thought that he sholde poison beye,
With which he mighte sleen his felawes tweye;   560
For-why the feend foond him in swich livinge
That he hadde leve him to sorwe bringe.
For this was outrely his fulle entente,
To sleen hem bothe, and nevere to repente.
And forth he gooth, no lenger wolde he tarie,
Into the toun, unto a pothecarie,
And preyde him that he him wolde selle
Som poison, that he mighte his rattes quelle;
And eek ther was a polcat in his hawe,
That, as he seyde, his capouns hadde yslawe,   570
And fain he wolde wreke him, if he mighte,
On vermin that destroyed him by nighte.

The pothecarie answerde, 'And thou shalt have
A thing that, also God my soule save,
In al this world ther is no creature,
That eten or dronken hath of this confiture
Noght but the montance of a corn of whete,
That he ne shal his lif anon forlete;
Ye, sterve he shal, and that in lasse while
Than thou wolt goon a paas nat but a mile,   580
This poisoun is so strong and violent.'

This cursed man hath in his hond yhent
This poisoun in a box, and sith he ran
Into the nexte strete unto a man,
And borwed of him large botelles thre;
And in the two his poison poured he;
The thridde he kepte clene for his drinke.
For al the night he shoop him for to swinke

In caryinge of the gold out of that place.
590 And whan this riotour, with sory grace,
Hadde filled with wyn his grete botels thre,
To his felawes again repaireth he.

What nedeth it to sermone of it moore?
For right as they hadde cast his deeth bifoore,
Right so they han him slain, and that anon.
And whan that this was doon, thus spak that oon:
'Now lat us sitte and drinke, and make us merie,
And afterward we wol his body berie.'
And with that word it happed him, par cas,
600 To take the botel ther the poison was,
And drank, and yaf his felawe drinke also,
For which anon they storven bothe two.

But certes, I suppose that Avycen
Wroot nevere in no canon, ne in no fen,
Mo wonder signes of empoisoning
Than hadde thise wrecches two, er hir ending.
Thus ended been thise homicides two,
And eek the false empoisonere also.

O cursed sinne of alle cursednesse!
610 O traitours homicide, O wikkednesse!
O glotonye, luxurie, and hasardrye!
Thou blasphemour of Crist with vileynye
And othes grete, of usage and of pride!
Allas! mankinde, how may it bitide
That to thy creatour, which that the wroghte,
And with his precious herte-blood thee boghte,
Thou art so fals and so unkinde, allas?

Now, goode men, God foryeve yow youre trespas,
And ware yow fro the sinne of avarice!
620 Myn hooly pardoun may yow alle warice,

So that ye offre nobles or sterlinges,
Or elles silver broches, spoones, ringes.
Boweth youre heed under this hooly bulle!
Cometh up, ye wives, offreth of youre wolle!
Youre names I entre heer in my rolle anon;
Into the blisse of hevene shul ye gon.
I yow assoille by myn heigh power,
Yow that wol offre, as clene and eek as cleer
As ye were born.—And lo, sires, thus I preche.
And Jhesu Crist, that is oure soules leche,   630
So graunte yow his pardoun to receive,
For that is best; I wol yow nat deceive.
    But sires, o word forgat I in my tale:
I have relikes and pardoun in my male
As faire as any man in Engelond,
Whiche were me yeven by the popes hond.
If any of yow wole, of devocion,
Offren, and han myn absolucion,
Com forth anon, and kneleth heere adoun,
And mekely receiveth my pardoun;   640
Or elles taketh pardoun as ye wende,
Al newe and fressh at every miles ende,
So that ye offren, alwey newe and newe,
Nobles or pens, whiche that be goode and trewe.
It is an honour to everich that is heer
That ye mowe have a suffisant pardoneer
T'assoille yow, in contree as ye ride,
For aventures whiche that may bitide.
Paraventure ther may fallen oon or two
Doun of his hors, and breke his nekke atwo.   650
Looke which a seuretee is it to yow alle
That I am in youre felaweshipe yfalle,

75   6-2

That may assoille yow, bothe moore and lasse,
Whan that the soule shal fro the body passe.
I rede that oure Hoost heere shal biginne,
For he is moost envoluped in sinne.
Com forth, sire Hoost, and offre first anon,
And thou shalt kisse the relikes everychon,
Ye, for a grote! Unbokele anon thy purs.
660   'Nay, nay,' quod he, 'thanne have I Cristes curs!
Lat be,' quod he, 'it shal nat be, so theech!
Thou woldest make me kisse thyn olde breech,
And swere it were a relik of a seint,
Though it were with thy fundement depeint!
But, by the crois which that Seint Eleyne fond
I wolde I hadde thy coillons in myn hond
In stide of relikes or of seintuarie.
Lat kutte hem of, I wol thee helpe hem carie;
They shul be shrined in an hogges toord!'
670   This Pardoner answerde nat a word;
So wrooth he was, no word ne wolde he seye.
    'Now,' quod oure Hoost, 'I wol no lenger pleye
With thee, ne with noon oother angry man.'
But right anon the worthy Knight bigan,
Whan that he saugh that al the peple lough,
'Namoore of this, for it is right ynough.
Sire Pardoner, be glad and myrie of cheere;
And ye, sire Hoost, that been to me so deere,
I prey yow that ye kisse the Pardoner.
680   And Pardoner, I prey thee, drawe thee neer,
And, as we diden, lat us laughe and pleye.'
Anon they kiste, and riden forth hir weye.

NOTES

1–16. The Host is referring to the tale just told by the Physician, in which a wicked magistrate (*fals justise*) attempted, with the help of a *fals cherl*, to seduce the beautiful and virtuous daughter of a knight, but was prevented by her father's killing her. Here and elsewhere, Harry Bailly responds to the tales told by the pilgrims with a ready flow of emotion.

1. *as* 'as if'.

2. *by nailes and by blood* An oath by the nails with which Christ was fastened to the cross (or possibly His own finger-nails) and by the blood which He shed on it. Here and in line 28 below we are already being prepared for the blasphemies of *The Pardoner's Tale*.

4. *herte* 'the human mind'.

5. *thise* 'all such'.

7. *to deere boughte she beautee* 'she paid too high a price for her beauty'.

8. *al day* 'always'.

9. *yiftes of Fortune and of Nature* The gifts of Nature were natural endowments of the mind and body (e.g. intelligence and beauty); those of Fortune were outward circumstances such as wealth and social rank. The girl in *The Physician's Tale* possessed both.

13–14. 'People very often receive more harm than benefit from both the gifts I am now referring to.'

17. *passe over, is no fors* 'let us pass over it, it does not matter'.

19–21. The Host is proudly showing off his knowledge of medical terms, but the word *galiones* has not been found elsewhere, and so perhaps he has made a mistake: he may not know as much as he likes to think. The same is true of the word *cardynacle* in line 27.

22. 'God and our Lady Saint Mary bless them.'

23. 'As I hope to prosper, you are a fine-looking man.' *So moot I theen* is a common asseveration, with no exact equivalent in modern speech.

24. *Ronyan* It is not known whether this is St Ronan or St Ninian. The word is pronounced with three syllables here, but with two in line 34 below.

25. *in terme* 'in your technical language'. The Host is being mock-modest: he has just been trying to show that he *can* speak *in terme*.

26. *thou doost myn herte to erme* 'you make my heart grieve'.

28. *by Corpus bones!* 'by God's bones!'. This is a common oath of Harry's. *But* here is 'unless'.

32. *beel ami* 'good fellow'. A courteous address, taken from the French, the language of medieval courtliness, and perhaps used ironically here.

37–40. Chaucer, like other medieval writers, normally assumes that literary taste follows class distinction; *gentils* (aristocratic people, such as the Knight, the Squire, the Prioress, etc.) will prefer *som moral thing*, while a *cherl* (a person of low class, such as the Pardoner or Miller) will prefer *ribaudye* (filth).

42. *that* Used redundantly, as here, in many relative constructions. Compare *whennes that I come* in line 49 and *Which that was of an hooly Jewes sheep* in line 65.

44–5. 'I take pains to speak loudly, and to make my sermon ring out as sonorously as a bell.' There is perhaps an unspoken irony in the use of a bell, a religious warning, as a simile to describe something irreligious; compare the remark that the Monk's bridle jingled in the wind as loudly and clearly as the chapel bell (*General Prologue*, 170–1).

47. 'My text is always the same, and always has been.' *Theme* is a technical term of the medieval *ars praedicandi*.

48. 'The love of money is the root of all evils' (St Paul's first Epistle to Timothy vi. 10).

50. *bulles* 'official documents with seals attached'.
    Alle and some 'each and every one'.

51. *oure lige lordes seel* This refers to the seal of the bishop who licensed the Pardoner.

52. *my body to warente* 'to protect myself'.

55. *telle I forth my tales* 'I repeat what I have to say'.

56–7. After establishing his right to preach with a presumably genuine document, the Pardoner goes on to dazzle his audience with others which are more likely to be forgeries.

59. *to saffron with my predicacioun* 'with which to give flavour and colour to my sermon'. Saffron is a plant still used in cooking to give a yellow colour and a distinctive taste. The culinary metaphor is a good sign of the Pardoner's attitude towards his sermons: he thinks of them as dishes concocted to impress his congregation.

60. *hem* A wealth of contempt is expressed in this single word, the first reference to his congregation.

61. *cristal stones* Glass boxes, such as religious relics are still sometimes kept in.

64. *latoun* This is an alloy of copper and zinc.

65. *an hooly Jewes sheep* The holy Jew was no doubt meant to suggest some Old Testament figure.

69. 'That has eaten or been stung by any creeping creature.' *Worm* was used in Chaucer's time to refer to snakes or insects as well as worms.

72. *of pokkes and of scabbe* These are skin-diseases of sheep.

75. 'If the master who owns the animals.'

81. *jalous rage* 'a frenzy of jealousy'.

82. 'Let his soup be made with this water.'

85. 'Although she had taken two or three priests as her lovers.' In this last few lines the Pardoner has been playing to his audience like an experienced comedian. The suggestion of a 'cure' for jealousy is likely to be met with a murmur of amusement, arising from the assumption that wives *are* unfaithful; the idea that the 'cure' will work even though the husband *knows* of the infidelity will perhaps produce open laughter; and finally the Pardoner cuts across this with his sudden dig at the immorality of priests, to produce a culminating outburst of laughter.

86. *miteyn* A medieval farmer would use a mitten for sowing seed, since this work had to be done by hand.

90. *so that* 'so long as'. Here the Pardoner first lets his *cupiditas* appear openly.

92–8. This apparently altruistic warning will in fact increase the Pardoner's receipts rather than diminish them, because anyone who does not make an offering will naturally be suspected of being in a state of mortal sin.

93. *that he* 'of such a kind that he'.

98. *offren* 'make an offering' (of money or goods).

99. 'And whoever finds himself free from such a fault.'

104. *an hundred mark* One mark was worth 13*s.* 4*d.* (that is, two-thirds of £1), and, since in the fourteenth century money was worth much more than it is now, a hundred marks a year would have been an enormous income.

106. *lewed* 'lay'—not *clerks*, such as the Pardoner pretends to be, and therefore ignorant. In the earlier Middle Ages, literacy, and hence learning, had been almost entirely confined

to those in ecclesiastical orders. See Appendix to *An Intro-duction to Chaucer*.

110–11. One of the many similes taken by Chaucer from country life, a field of experience which was familiar even to town-dwellers in his own day (because even the largest English towns were very small), but which is likely to be less familiar nowadays. Compare *goon a-blakeberied* in line 120 below.

113. *bisynesse* 'how active I am' (not the modern 'business'). The delight expressed here in the completeness or full-bloodedness of an activity is characteristic of Chaucer, and not just of the Pardoner. In *The Canon's Yeoman's Prologue*, for example, he says of the Canon, who has just ridden up at a great pace, 'But it was joye for to seen him swete!'.

117. *nat but for* 'only'.

118. *nothing* 'not at all'. (It has the same meaning in line 147 below.)

119. *nevere* 'not at all'.

120. *goon a-blakeberied* This means to go wandering all over the place, like someone picking blackberries: a euphemistic way of saying that he does not care if they are damned, once he has their money.

123. 'Some in order to please people and flatter them.'

126. *for* This conjunction seems to indicate that the Pardoner is momentarily classing himself with those who preach well out of hatred, even though his main claim is that he preaches for gain. There is certainly an element of blank malignity, evil for its own sake, in his blasphemous way of life.

127. *him* Someone in his imaginary congregation. Compare the contemptuous *hem* in line 60 above. The image of the Pardoner as a poisonous snake is picked up again in the mention of his spitting out venom in line 135 below.

130. *my bretheren* The Pardoner seems to think of pardoners in general as forming a brotherhood, almost as if they belonged to a religious order like the friars. In fact, *quaestores* were accused by Pope Boniface IX of forming associations to deceive the public, so this turn of phrase may be another sign of Chaucer's accuracy.

134. *doon us displesances* 'do things that displease us'.

137. The explicitness about literary purpose and structure found in this line and in line 148 below—saying what one is going to do, and then saying that one has finished doing it—is

characteristic of medieval poetry. It arises from the fact that it was normally delivered to an audience of listeners (like the pilgrims), who would not possess copies of what they were listening to, and would need to have its internal structural divisions made clear to them. In a written work these could be indicated by paragraphs and sub-headings.

148. 'That ought to be enough on this subject.'

149. *ensamples* Like *theme*, this is a technical term, meaning stories told to illustrate or support some general moral. *Ensamples* were extremely common in medieval sermons.

152. *reporte and holde* 'repeat and keep in their minds'. This of course was the main purpose of *ensamples* in preaching, though the Pardoner mentions it as part of his contempt for his congregations.

154. *for I teche* 'through my teaching'.

156. *I thoghte it nevere* 'I have never intended that'.

159. *make baskettes* St Paul the Hermit made baskets for a living, but Chaucer may have confused him with the apostle St Paul, since the Pardoner immediately afterwards says that he is determined not to imitate any of the apostles.

162–7. There is a relish in these details, as the Pardoner boasts of his sensual egotism, into which one cannot help entering. It is indeed this energy in his evil nature which enables Chaucer to make a study in moral corruption partly comic. One might compare Shakespeare's presentation of Richard in *Richard III*.

166. *licour of the vine* 'juice of the grape'—i.e. wine.

167. A vain boast. See Introduction, p. 15.

172. *by reson* 'if you are reasonable'.

173–4. The paradox that an evil man can tell a tale which is genuinely moral in its effect is striking. See Introduction, pp. 25–6.

176. *now hoold youre pees* Another sign of a listening audience. Medieval poetry is full of requests for silence and attention, which were very necessary when literature fulfilled a social function as one among many means of communal entertainment.

177. *whilom* This placing of the story in an indefinite past is used at the beginning of many of *The Canterbury Tales*. It is roughly the equivalent of the fairy story 'once upon a time'.

180. *as* This word is redundant.

   lutes, and giternes These were both stringed instruments of the same basic type as the modern guitar.

182. *over hir might* 'more than they could hold'.

183–5. Here the tavern is presented as a temple of the devil, in which a blasphemous worship is carried on in the form of gluttony.

185. *abhominable* An 'h' was mistakenly introduced into this word, on the assumption that it was taken from the Latin *ab homine*, 'away from (the true nature of) man'. It thus has a stronger sense than now, meaning 'revoltingly unnatural' or 'bestial'.

188–9. Swearing by the different parts of Christ's body was a common form of verbal blasphemy in the Middle Ages, of which many examples are found in *The Pardoner's Prologue and Tale*. There was a recurrent ecclesiastical campaign against it, and it was often represented by its opponents, as here, as a 'recrucifixion' of Christ.

189. *hem thoughte* 'it seemed to them'. Antisemitism was a persistent element in medieval Christianity, and aroused less horror in Chaucer's time than it does now. The Jewish people were held collectively responsible for the murder of Christ, and in England they were isolated into ghettoes, persecuted, heavily taxed, and finally expelled from the country in 1290. Christian antisemitism is expressed exultantly in *The Prioress's Tale*, in which a little Christian boy is brutally murdered by Jews (ritual murder of children was a favourite accusation against them), and his murderers are eventually tortured and killed.

191. *tombesteres* 'dancing-girls'. There is some doubt whether the *-ster* ending (as in the modern *spinster*) always indicated a female person in Middle English. Here, in the light of *fetys and smale*, it clearly does.

194–5. *whiche been...kindle* 'who are the true servants of the devil, charged with kindling'.

196. A main theme of this section on the sins is the interdependence of the sins: to commit one is to commit all the rest, and all are forms of blasphemy. Thus any sin becomes supremely horrifying and fascinatingly important, and the sinner is drawn into the great drama of the universe, in which God and the devil are locked in mortal combat.

197. 'I take the Bible as my witness.'

198. This line is based on a mistranslation of 'hooly writ'. The Latin text (of St Paul's Epistle to the Ephesians v. 18) reads: 'Nolite inebriari vino, in quo est luxuria' ('Do not become

82

drunk with wine, in which is excess'), but *luxuria* was taken to have the specialized medieval sense of 'sexual excess'. The reference to an authoritative text in support of a statement of one's own is typical of medieval literature, and especially of the medieval sermon, where the authority is usually Scriptural. A series of such references follows, and the Pardoner does not take up his story again until line 375. The 'interlude' is not irrelevant however; see Introduction, p. 32.

199. *dronken Looth* See Genesis xix. 30–6.

202. *whoso wel the stories soghte* 'as anyone who had looked carefully through the histories would know'. *The stories* may be the Biblical accounts of Herod and John the Baptist (Matthew xiv and Mark vi), or possibly the *Historia Evangelica* of Peter Comestor, a favourite source-book for Scriptural *exempla*.

205. *ful giltelees* 'although he was completely innocent'.

206. 'Seneca makes a good remark, undoubtedly.' Seneca was a Latin writer of the first century A.D., a Stoic philosopher and a dramatist, who was greatly admired in the Middle Ages. The remark quoted by the Pardoner comes from one of his letters.

210. *yfallen in a shrewe* 'when it occurs in some miserable creature'.

212–14. Invocation of a person or thing not actually present is part of the rhetorical technique of the medieval art of poetry; the technical name for it is *exclamatio* or *apostrophatio*. The aim is usually, as here, to stir up emotion in the audience. The *oure...oure...us* refers to the whole human race, damned, as the Pardoner goes on to explain, by Adam's sin of gluttony.

215. *boght us with his blood again* 'redeemed us with His blood'.

221. *it is no drede* 'there is no doubt'.

222. *as I rede* The Pardoner is in fact drawing on a written source for this idea, which sounds somewhat odd to modern ears, that the eating of the forbidden fruit could be classified as an act of gluttony. The source is St Jerome's *Adversus Jovinianum.*

226. *on thee wel oghte us pleyne* 'we ought indeed to complain against you'.

227. *wiste a man* 'if one knew'.

231. *the shorte throte* A compressed and concrete way of referring to the short time during which the food is still

providing enjoyment, before it reaches the stomach. Here and later the Pardoner presents gluttony not as a moral abstraction but in terms of the physical sensations and activities involved in it—the mouth, the gullet, the throat, and the bustling cooks who labour to provide their brief satisfactions. Gluttony, like the other sins he deals with, thus becomes extraordinarily vivid—repulsive in a way which makes the reader's gorge rise, and yet at the same time irresistibly fascinating.

232–3. The grammatical construction is confused by the enumeration of details (east, west, north, south, etc.), so that *maketh that* is followed not by the subjunctive one would expect, but by the infinitive *to swinke*.

236–7. The quotation from St Paul comes from the 1st Epistle to the Corinthians vi. 13: 'Meats for the belly, and the belly for meats: but God shall destroy both it and them'.

240. *white and rede* 'white and red wines' (compare line 276 below).

241. This strikingly contracted image comes from the *Adversus Jovinianum*.

243. *the apostel* This is St Paul again, the Epistle to the Philippians iii. 18–19: 'For many walk, of whom I have told you often, and now tell you even weeping, that they are the enemies of the cross of Christ: Whose end is destruction, whose God is their belly'.

247. *of whiche* 'whose'. In this line gluttony is again treated as a form of blasphemy, as in lines 183–5 above.

248. The irregular rhythm of this line provides for dramatic pauses between the different names for the belly.

251. *is thee to finde* 'it is to provide for you'.

252. *thise* Used to indicate familiarity with the ways of cooks, not to distinguish any particular group of cooks. *Streyne* is perhaps used in a double sense: 'exert themselves' (connecting it with *stampe*) and 'pass things through strainers' (connecting it with *grinde*). The following remarks on gluttony are borrowed from part of the *De Contemptu Mundi*, by Pope Innocent III.

253. A 'metaphysical' image, borrowed from Innocent III, which plays with the technical language of medieval philosophy. In this language *accidents* are external characteristics (e.g. redness, hardness, coldness) and *substaunce* is the supposed essence underlying these. Thus the Pardoner means that the

cooks so completely transform the external qualities of their ingredients that no one could tell what 'substaunce' their dishes are made of. But the line may also include a blasphemous parody of the Catholic doctrine that in the Mass the bread and wine are 'trans-substantiated' into the body and blood of Christ, despite their retaining the 'accidents' of ordinary bread and wine. In Chaucer's own time this doctrine had been denied by John Wyclif, so that it was a controversial matter, to which an allusion would quickly be picked up.

257. When spoken, this line has a repulsively slippery sound, which perfectly conveys a sense of the sliding of soft, rich food down the throat.

259. 'The glutton's sauce shall be made for his delight.'

260. 'To renew his appetite continually.'

261–2. Another quotation from St Paul (1st Epistle to Timothy v. 6): 'But she that liveth in pleasure is dead while she liveth'.

263. At this point the Pardoner turns from gluttony in general to speak of the special form of gluttony that leads to drunkenness. There is also a change of tone—essential if the audience's interest is to be held—from portentous denunciation to coarse humour with a more direct appeal.

268. *Sampsoun* An imitation of a drunkard's heavy snoring, which in the next line provides an unexpected and telling moral point.

270. *as it were a stiked swyn* 'like a stuck pig'.

274. *in whom that* 'the man in whom'.

276. *kepe yow fro* 'keep yourselves away from'.

278. Fish Street and Cheapside, both of which still exist, were part of the shopping centre of medieval London. Chaucer's father, who was a wine merchant (hence, no doubt, Chaucer's apparently expert knowledge), lived in Thames Street, from which Fish Street leads out.

   To selle 'for sale'.

279–80. These lines are perhaps said with a wink. The Pardoner is jokingly suggesting that Spanish wine from *Lepe* is to be found mixed with wine from the South of France (*Rochele* or *Burdeux* in line 285) because the vineyards are close together. In fact it is because the wine merchants dilute expensive French wines with cheap Spanish ones. The result is heady.

281. *fumositee* According to medieval physiology, the contents of the stomach could produce vapours which literally 'went

to one's head', and produced dreams or the symptoms of drunkenness.

288. *dar I seye* 'I have no hesitation in saying'.

293. *looke* A common way of introducing an *exemplum*.

293–5. Attila, king of the tribe of Huns, died in bed after a drunken debauch on his wedding night.

300–1. 'Read the Bible, and see what is explicitly said there about giving wine to those who administer justice.' The reference is to Proverbs xxxi. 4–5: 'It is not for kings, O Lemuel, it is not for kings to drink wine; nor for princes strong drink: Lest they drink, and forget the law, and pervert the judgment of any of the afflicted'.

303–4. The Pardoner is getting into his stride, and is determined to leave no sin mentioned in his story without its sermon.

307–8. The anti-climax of the descent from murder to time-wasting is no doubt deliberate. See Introduction, p. 30.

317–34. This *exemplum*, and the attack on gambling which it illustrates, are both taken from a Latin work by a twelfth-century English writer, the *Policraticus* of John of Salisbury. According to John the ambassador's name was 'Chilon'.

319. *make hire alliaunce* 'make an alliance with the Corinthians'.

329–30. 'For, on my honour, I would rather die than ally you to gamblers.'

336. *the book* The *Policraticus*.

337. *him* This word is redundant.

346. *fals swering* 'swearing oaths that one does not intend to keep'.

348. *Mathew* The reference is to Matthew v. 33–4: 'Again, ye have heard that it hath been said by them of old time, Thou shalt not forswear thyself, but shalt perform unto the Lord thine oaths: But I say unto you, Swear not at all'.

350–1. The quotation is from Jeremiah iv. 2: 'And thou shalt swear, The Lord liveth, in truth, in judgment, and in righteousness'.

351. *in doom* That is, when a formal oath is required, as in a court of law.

353. *firste table* The first five of the Ten Commandments given by God to Moses.

355. *seconde heeste* The second according to the Roman Catholic division; the third according to the Protestant division.

359. *as by ordre* 'according to the order of the Commandments'.

360. 'One who understands His commandments knows.'

Notes

363–4. From Ecclesiasticus xxiii. 11: 'If he swear in vain, he shall not be innocent, but his house shall be full of calamities'.

365. *nailes* See note on line 2.

366. The abbey of Hales in Gloucestershire possessed a phial which was supposed to contain some of Christ's blood.

367. This line uses the technical jargon of medieval gambling. In the game of *hasard*, a *chaunce* is a dice-throw which neither loses nor wins, but enables the thrower to have another turn. French numbers (as *cynk* and *treye*) were used for the six faces of the dice.

370. *bones two* 'dice'.

375. The Pardoner now at last turns back from his sermon to the story which exemplifies the sins he has been preaching against. And once he has started, he leaps to the heart of the story with masterly abruptness. *Of whiche I telle* may be in the future tense ('of whom I am going to tell you'), but the *riotoures* have not been mentioned before, and this opening implies a familiarity which does not really exist.

376. *prime* This is one of the seven canonical hours, the times appointed by the Church for prayer. It means about six in the morning, but by mentioning the time Chaucer reminds us of the divine context in which this revelry is set: service begins early in the *develes temple*.

377. *were set hem* 'had sat themselves down'.

378. A bell was carried along in front of the corpse at a funeral.

380. *that oon of hem gan callen* 'one of them called'.

387. *to-night* 'this last night'.

388. The irregularity of rhythm in this line throws a meaningful emphasis on *fordronke*.

389. In this line the long repeated *ee*'s and *th* sounds horribly suggest the slithering approach of death, and at the same time the awed whisper in which the boy mentions him.

393. *this pestilence* 'during this plague'. Medieval England was periodically ravaged by plagues—hence the matter-of-factness of this reference.

401. *henne over a mile* 'over a mile from here'.

406. *Goddes armes* The first of the many oaths by parts of God's body that the Pardoner has warned us to expect.

408. *by wey and eek by strete* 'through highways and by-ways'.

411. They raise their hands ceremonially as they take the oath of brotherhood.

418. *ybore brother* 'brother by birth'.

425. *nat fully* 'almost'.

426. *wolde han troden* 'were going to step'.

427. On the identity and function in the story of this mysterious old man, see Introduction, pp. 37–40.

431. *with sory grace!* 'bad luck to you!'.

436. *into Inde* This is a common formula in medieval poetry, standing for 'to the end of the earth'.

441–52. Compare Revelation ix. 6: 'And in those days shall men seek death, and shall not find it; and shall desire to die, and death shall flee from them'.

443–4. The ground is his mother's gate because the earth is his mother. Thus the tapping of his walking-stick is presented as a request for re-admittance to the earth that bore him.

448–50. The old man means that he wishes he could exchange his *cheste* full of clothes for the shroud in which he will be buried.

453–4. *curteisye...vileynye* These words are traditional opposites, meaning the behaviour that one would expect of a courtly person and of an uncultivated lower-class person (a *vilein*) respectively. See Appendix to *An Introduction to Chaucer*.

457–8. The quotation is from Leviticus xix. 32: 'Thou shalt rise up before the hoary head, and honour the face of the old man'.

461. For *if* Chaucer may have written *yif*, an older form of the same word which is found in some manuscripts; this would prevent an elision between *age* and *if* from making the line too short. But a hiatus instead of an elision between the two words would provide a significant pause before the sinister irony of the old man's doubt: 'In age—if that ye so longe abide'.

462. More irony: God will indeed be with the revellers, and will pass judgement on them, though they disregard His presence.

463. This line suggests another element in the mystery surrounding the old man: he has a destination, but where is not disclosed.

469. *have heer my trouthe* 'take my word'.

475. *croked wey* The crookedness of the path which will lead them to Death is of course symbolic: it is the path of sin.

480–1. *God save...yow amende* 'God, who redeemed mankind, preserve you and make you better'.

484. *florins* A florin was worth half a mark, or 6*s*. 8*d*., in Chaucer's time.

485. *wel ny an eighte busshels* 'something like eight bushels'.

493–4. Compare the Host's remark in lines 8–10 that the gifts of Fortune often bring death: the reveller has no grounds for his confidence.

495. 'And we will spend it as easily as it has come to us.' Compare the proverb, 'Lightly come, lightly go'.

498–501. *mighte this gold...thanne were we* 'if this gold might ...then we would be'.

499. His first words betray his immediate thought—to keep the gold for himself—but he quickly corrects them and glosses over his mistake with an assurance that the gold belongs, of course, to all of them.

501. *heigh felicitee* 'supreme happiness'. The phrase has a theological flavour: *felicitee* tends to be applied to the blessedness of heaven, and the reveller is mistaking the nature of true happiness.

504. *doon us honge* 'have us hanged'.

507–8. He is proposing that someone should hold out a number of straws in his hand, each should draw one out, and the person who draws the shortest should have to go and fetch provisions for them. This was a common way of drawing lots in medieval times; it is the method the Host suggests in *The General Prologue* for deciding who should tell the first tale.

508. *lat se wher* 'let us see on whom'.

509. *with herte blithe* The idea seems to be 'willingly, without grumbling about it'; but the phrase is little more than a tag.

515. *by oon assent* 'by agreement among us all'.

516. *that oon* 'one'; compare *that oon* and *that oother* in line 521.

523. *thy profit* 'something that will do you good'.

525. *and that ful greet plentee* 'and a vast amount of it too'.

529. 'Wouldn't I have done you a friendly turn?'

546. *my deere freend* The parenthetic placing of this phrase, along with its long *ee* sounds, effectively suggests cunning.

548. *right at oure owene wille* 'exactly as we please'.

554. *if so were* 'if it should come about'.

563. 'For his fixed intention was definitely.'

569. *polcat* A small animal like a weasel, now rare in England, but more common in Chaucer's time.

571. 'And he was eager to take vengeance if he could.'
572. *vermin* For the chemist this means the rats and th polecat, but the reveller is contemptuously applying the term to his companions, not knowing that they are in fact intending to 'destroy' him.
574. *also God my soule save* 'as I hope to be saved'.
576–8. 'Who, after eating or drinking an amount of thi preparation the size of a grain of wheat, will not immediately lose his life.'
579–80. *and that...a mile* 'and that in less time than it wil take you to walk a mile at normal speed'. The chemist use images of a very immediate kind: it is unpleasantly easy to imagine the amount needed of the poison, and the exact time it takes to work.
583. *he ran* This is only one of many indications of violent speed in the Tale. See Introduction, pp. 35–7.
593. *sermone of* 'talk on about'. The word *sermone* does no necessarily imply actual preaching.
597–8. The jaunty rhythm of this couplet is intentionally jarring: the revellers have no idea what fate they are on the brink of.
602. The final stages of the Tale are presented in a deliberately flat, laconic way, and in this line the very syntax conspires to underplay the climax, by mentioning the last two deaths in a subordinate clause, almost as if they were only an afterthought
603. *Avycen* Avicenna, the Latinized form of the name of Ibr Sina, the great Arabic philosopher and scientist. He was wel known in the West as an authority on medicine.
604. *canon...fen* Avicenna's chief work, the *Book of the Canon in Medicine*, was divided into sections called *fens*, and it often uses the term *canon* in chapter-headings to mean 'rule of procedure'.
610. *traitours homicide* 'murderous betrayers'.
612. *Thou blasphemour* This presumably refers to 'synne', but the Pardoner is now no doubt running his eyes over his audience.
615. *which that the wroghte* 'who made you'.
619. *avarice* The transition is now complete from the unmiti-gated horror of the Tale itself to the Pardoner's usual roguery.
621. *nobles or sterlinges* i.e. gold or silver.
630–2. For interpretative comment on these lines, see Intro-duction, pp. 46–8.

Notes

1. *so graunte* 'grant'.

2. *al newe and fressh* He speaks of pardon as if it were something physically delightful, such as a cake. Compare the description of the Pardoner's wallet in *The General Prologue* as 'Bretful of pardoun, comen from Rome al hoot'.

9-50. He seems to take a positive delight in the possibility: not just one of them may break his neck, but one or two.

1. *looke which a seuretee* 'think what a safeguard'.

2-3. 'That I have fallen into company with you—I who can absolve you, whatever your rank.'

0-9. This coarse outspokenness is characteristic of the Host. He is a powerful man, who is dominated by none of the pilgrims, but only by his wife.

0. *thanne have I Cristes curs* 'may I be cursed by Christ if I do'.

1. *so theech* 'as I may prosper'.

5. St Helena, the mother of Constantine the Great, was supposed to have discovered the actual cross on which Christ was crucified.

8. *lat kutte hem of* 'have them cut off'. The Host's coarseness has indeed a sharp edge; Chaucer in *The General Prologue* has said that the Pardoner is a eunuch.

74-81. The Knight is the person of highest social rank on the pilgrimage, so he is in a position to act as arbitrator in quarrels; and since he is a good-natured man, and takes seriously the responsibilities of his rank, he often does so.

76. *right ynough* 'quite enough'.

79-80. *I prey yow...I prey thee* According to the manuscript on which this text is based, the Knight addresses the Host with the respectful plural form, and the Pardoner with the familiar singular. For this distinction, see *An Introduction to Chaucer*, p. 95.

APPENDIX

THE PORTRAIT OF THE PARDONER
IN 'THE GENERAL PROLOGUE'
lines 671–716

    With him ther rood a gentil PARDONER
Of Rouncivale, his freend and his compeer,
That streight was comen fro the court of Rome.
Ful loude he soong 'Com hider, love, to me!'
This Somonour bar to him a stif burdoun;
Was nevere trompe of half so greet a soun.
This Pardoner hadde heer as yelow as wex,
But smothe it heeng as dooth a strike of flex;
By ounces henge his lokkes that he hadde,
And therwith he his shuldres overspradde;
But thinne it lay, by colpons oon and oon.
But hood, for jolitee, wered he noon,
For it was trussed up in his walet.
Him thoughte he rood al of the newe jet;
Dischevelee, save his cappe, he rood al bare.
Swiche glaringe eyen hadde he as an hare.
A vernicle hadde he sowed upon his cappe.
His walet lay biforn him in his lappe,
Bretful of pardoun, comen from Rome al hoot.
A voys he hadde as smal as hath a goot.
No berd hadde he, ne nevere sholde have;
As smothe it was as it were late shave.
I trowe he were a gelding or a mare.
But of his craft, fro Berwik into Ware,
Ne was ther swich another pardoner.

For in his male he hadde a pilwe-beer,
Which that he seyde was Oure Lady veil:
He seyde he hadde a gobet of the seil
That Seint Peter hadde, whan that he wente
Upon the see, til Jhesu Crist him hente.
He hadde a crois of latoun ful of stones,
And in a glas he hadde pigges bones.
But with thise relikes, whan that he fond
A povre person dwellinge upon lond,
Upon a day he gat him moore moneye
Than that the person gat in monthes tweye;
And thus, with feyned flaterye and japes,
He made the person and the peple his apes.
But trewely to tellen atte laste,
He was in chirche a noble ecclesiaste.
Wel koude he rede a lessoun or a storie,
But alderbest he song an offertorie;
For wel he wiste, whan that song was songe,
He moste preche and wel affile his tonge
To winne silver, as he ful wel koude;
Therefore he song the murierly and loude.

GLOSSARY

abhominable unnatural (see note on l. 185)

abide (inf. *abiden*) (l. 461) endure; (l. 477) wait

a-blakeberied wandering about

aboght (inf. *abyen*) paid for

abye (inf. *abyen*) pay for

accident see note on l. 253

acorded (inf. *acorden*) come to an agreement

actes deeds

adoun down

advocas lawyers

again (l. 141) against; (l. 431) back

agains in the presence of

ago(o)n past; (l. 524) gone

al (as conjunction, followed by subjunctive verb) although

alestake inn signpost

algate all the same

allyen (sometimes reflexive) make alliance with

also (l. 520) as

alwey always

amende (inf. *amenden*) make better, reform

ami companion

amis wrongly

annexed attached

anon at once

artow art thou

as (ll. 1, 543) as if; (l. 179) such as

assent (l. 472) conspiracy; (l. 515) agreement

assoille (inf. *assoillen*) absolve

asterte (inf. *asterten*) avoid

atte at the

Attilla Attila, king of the Huns

atwo in two pieces

auctoritee authority

avaunced promoted

aventures accidents

avised (inf. *avisen*) prepared

aviseth yow (inf. *avisen*) consider

avow (l. 409) *make avow* swear

Avycen Avicenna

axe (inf. *axen*) ask

ay always

bad (inf. *bidden*) told, ordered

baudes bawds, procurers

be (inf. *be(e)n*) been

be(e)n be, are

bekke (inf. *bekken*) nod the head

berie (inf. *berien*) bury

berne barn

bet (l. 381) quickly

beth (inf. *be(e)n*) be

beye (inf. *b(e)yen*) buy

bicched cursed

bicomen become

bifoore before

biforn before, in front of

bigan (inf. *biginnen*) began

bihoolde (inf. *biholden*) behold, look

bitide come to pass

bitwix between

bitwixen between

biwreye (inf. *biwreyen*) give away

blame fault

blaspheme blasphemy

blissed blessed

blithe gay

boght again (inf. *b(e)yen*) redeemed

boon bone

boost boasting

borwed (inf. *borwen*) borrowed

botel bottle

bo(u)ghte (inf. *b(e)yen*) (l. 7) paid for; (l. 616) redeemed

bourde (inf. *bourden*) joke

boyste box

breech breeches

breed bread

breke (inf. *breken*) break

broches brooches

bulle official document

Burdeux Bordeaux

but (ll. 28, 30, 455) unless

cake loaf of bread

cam (inf. *comen*) came

canon rule of procedure (see note to l. 604)

capitain commander

capouns capons (castrated cocks)

cardynacle heart-attack

carl fellow

cas, par cas by chance

cast (inf. *casten*) planned

catel goods, money

certes certainly

chambre room, bedroom

chaunce (l. 320) *par chaunce* by chance; (l. 367) see note

chaunge (inf. *chaungen*) exchange

cheere mood

Chepe Cheapside

cherl villain, lower-class person (see Appendix to *An Introduction to Chaucer*)

cheste clothes chest

citee city

cleer free from sin

clene clean

clepeth (inf. *clepen*) calls

clerk learned person, scholar, or one in holy orders (see Appendix to *An Introduction to Chaucer*)

clowt garment; (l. 450) shroud

clowtes rags

cod bag

coillons testicles

cokewold cuckold

comen (inf. *comen*) came

commune (l. 310) notorious; (l. 315) common

compaignye company, gang

comth (inf. *comen*) comes

confiture preparation

confusioun ruin

conseil secret

contree country

Corinthe Corinth

corn grain

corny tasting strongly of the corn it was made from

corrupt corrupted

cors (l. 18) body; (ll. 379, 382) corpse

countrefete (inf. *countrefeten*) imitate

coveitise covetousness

creatour creator

crepeth (inf. *crepen*) creeps

crois cross

croked crooked

cure care

curteisye courtesy (see also
  Appendix to *An Introduction
  to Chaucer*)
cut lot(s)
cynk five
dame mother
dampnable damnable
dampnacioun damnation
debate fight, attack
dede deed, act
deed dead
deere dear
dees dice
deeth death
defame dishonour, disgrace
defamed disgraced, slandered
defaute fault, lapse
deffended (inf. *deffenden*)
  forbidden
deffenden forbid
delices delights
delit delight
departed (inf. *departen*)
  divided
depeint stained
desolaat disgraced
destourbe (inf. *destourben*)
  hinder
destroyed (inf. *destroyen*)
  were preying on
devise (inf. *devisen*) describe
deyde (inf. *deyen*) died
deyntee delicate
diete food and drink
digne noble
dignitee glory
discrecioun judgement
dishonour injury
doghtres daughters
dominacioun domination
dong dung
doom judgement

doon (infinitive) do, cause;
  (past participle) done
dooth (inf. *doon*) do, does
doute doubt
doutelees undoubtedly
dowve dove, pigeon
drawe (inf. *drawen*) drawn
drede (ll. 221, 275) *it is no
  drede* there is no doubt
dronke(n) drunk
dronkelewe drunk
dronkenesse drunkenness
dyde (inf. *deyen*) died
ech each
echoon each one
eek also
eet (inf. *eten*) ate
Eleyne St Helena
elles else
embassadour ambassador
empoisonere poisoner
empoisoning poisoning
ensample illustrative stories
entencioun intention
entente purpose
entre (inf. *entren*) enter
envoluped enveloped
er before
erly early
erme grieve
erst er before
espye spy
est east
estaat social rank, position
eten (inf. *eten*) eaten
everemoore always
everich each (one)
expresly explicitly
fader father
fain willingly
fair good, fine
fals wicked, deceiving, lying

falsnesse deceit
faste (l. 280) close
feend devil
felawe companion
felaweshipe company
felicitee happiness
fen section (see note on
   l. 604)
fest fist
fetys neat, graceful
fey faith
fil (inf. *fallen*) fell
finde (inf. *finden*) (l. 251)
   provide for
Fisshstrete Fish Street
Flaundres Flanders
florin coin worth 6s. 8d.
folwen follow
fo(o)nd (inf. *finden*) found
for for, because
forbedeth (inf. *forbeden*)
   forbids
forby past
fordronke completely drunk
forgat (inf. *forgeten*) forgot
forlete (inf. *forleten*) lose
forswering perjury
forthermo furthermore
forther over moreover
for-why because
forwrapped wrapped up
foryeve (inf. *foryeven*)
   forgive
foul ugly, disgusting
free generous
fro from
frutesteres fruit-sellers
ful very, completely
fulfilled filled full
fumositee vapour (see note
   to l. 281)
fundement bottom

galiones ?drinks named after
   the physician Galen
gan (inf. *ginnen*) began; also
   used as an auxiliary to
   indicate the past tense
   (e.g. *gan callen* in l. 380,
   'called')
gaude trick
gentil noble
gentils upper-class people
   (see Appendix to *An
   Introduction to Chaucer*)
giltelees innocent
giternes citterns
glotonye gluttony; (l. 228)
   glotonies, cases of gluttony
glotoun glutton
golet gullet
gonne (inf. *ginnen*) began
good-man master
goon go, walk
governaunce government
grace favour, luck
graunte (inf. *graunten*)
   agree; (l. 631) grant
grete, greet great, large
grette (inf. *greten*) greeted
gretteste greatest
grisly horrifying
grote coin worth 4d.
habitacioun dwelling
han (inf. *ha(ve)n*) have
happed(e) (inf. *happen*) (it)
   occurred, befell
harrow! a cry of distress
hasardour gambler
hasard(rye) gambling
haunteden (inf. *haunten*)
   practised, gave themselves
   up to
haunteth (inf. *haunten*)
   practises

Glossary

hauteyn loud
hawe yard
Hayles Hales
heed head
heeld (inf. *holden*) considered, rated
heer here
heeste command(ment)
heigh(e) high
hem them(selves)
henne from here
hente (inf. *henten*) seize, catch
herkneth (inf. *herkneh*) listen (to)
Herodes Herod
herte heart
hevene heaven
hewe colour, appearance
heyre (made of) haircloth
hine labourer
hir their
hogges Hog's
holde (inf. *holden*) (l. 152) retain; (l. 310) considered
homicide (ll. 358, 371) murder; (l. 610) murderous
homicides (l. 607) murderers
hond hand
honest decent; (l. 271) *honeste cure*, self-respect
honge (inf. *hongen*) hang
honurable deserving reverence
hool cured
hooly writ the Bible
hoom home
hoor grey
hoord hoard
hope (inf. *hopen*) intend
idel vain
Inde India

ire anger
japes (l. 33) jokes; (l. 108) untrue stories
Jeremye Jeremiah
joliftee gaiety
jurdones chamber-pots
kaitif prisoner
kan (l. 46) know; (l. 527) can
kanstow? canst thou?
ke(e)p heed, notice
kepen guard, keep
kiste (inf. *kissen*) kissed
knave serving-boy
kneleth (inf. *knelen*) kneel
kutte (inf. *kutten*) cut
Lacidomye Lacedaemon, Sparta
lafte (inf. *leven*) left
Lamuel Lemuel
lasse less
lat (inf. *leten*) let
lat be give up
leche doctor, healer
lecherous causing lechery
leef desirous
leere (inf. *leeren*) learn
leet (inf. *leten*) let
leeve dear
lenger longer
Lepe a town in Spain
lese (inf. *lesen*) lose
lesinges lies
lete (inf. *leten*) give up
letuarie medicine
leve permission
levere rather, more willingly
lewed lay, ignorant (see Appendix to *An Introduction to Chaucer*)
licour juice
lightly easily
likerous greedy

Glossary

ivestow? (inf. *liven*) dost thou live?

livinge way of life

lond land

looke (inf. *looken*) consider (how); (ll. 540, 544) see to it

Looth Lot

lordinges (ladies and) gentlemen

lough (inf. *laughen*) laughed

lustes desires

luxurie lechery

lyf life

maister master, sir

maketh (inf. *maken*) (l. 232) causes

male bag

man (l. 240) one

maner kind of

mark money worth 13s. 4d.

mary marrow

Mathew St Matthew

matiere matter

mekely humbly

men people, one

mesurable (*of*) moderate (in)

mete food

might (l. 182) capacity

mirthe happiness

mistriste mistrust

mitayn, miteyn mitten

mo more

moiste fresh

montance amount

mooder mother

moore and lasse (l. 653) whatever your rank

moot (l. 23) may; (l. 41) must

moste must

mowe (inf. *mowen*) may

murye happily

myn my, mine

myrie pleasant, gay

namely especially

namoore no more

nat not

nathelees nevertheless

nay no

ne nor

nedeth (inf. *neden*) is necessary

nekke neck

never-a-deel not at all

nevere (l. 119) not at all

nobles gold coins worth 6s. 8d.

noght nothing, not, not at all

none, noon no

noot (inf. *witen*) do not know

nothing (l. 118) not at all

ny nearly

nyste (inf. *witen*) did not know

o one

of (l. 668) off

officeres servants

offren make an offering

offreth (inf. *offren*) offer

oghte (inf. *owen*) ought; (l. 226) *oghte us*, we ought

ones (l. 410) *al ones* at one

oon one

ooth oath

original origin

othes oaths

out of (l. 99) free from

outrely completely

over over, beyond

owene own

oweth (inf. *owen*) owns

paas (l. 580) *goon a paas* walk at normal speed

page servant

Glossary

paire set
paraventure perhaps
pardee indeed
parten depart
partest (inf. *parten*) (l. 466)
  shalt depart
Parthes Parthians
patente licence
Paul(us) St Paul
pens pennies
peple people
persevereth (inf. *perseveren*)
  lasts, endures
peyne me (inf. *peynen*) take
  pains
pitous(ly) piteous(ly)
plat flatly
plentee a large amount
plesance giving of pleasure
pleyen play, joke
pleyne (on) (inf. *pleynen*)
  complain (about), cry out
  (against)
plighte (inf. *plighten*) pledged
pokkes pocks
polcat polecat
policye ruling, administration
potage soup
pothecarie chemist
povereste poorest
povre poor
predicacioun preaching
prelat bishop, or other high
  ecclesiastic
preye (inf. *preyen*) beg, pray,
  request
preyere prayer
prince ruler
privee (l. 389) secret;
  (l. 241) lavatory
prively secretly
profit advantage

pronounce (inf. *pronouncen*)
  declare
propre own
prow benefit
quelle (inf. *quellen*) kill
quod (inf. *quethen*) said
quyte (inf. *quyten*) repay
rage fit of madness
rather sooner, earlier
rede (inf. *reden*) read;
  (ll. 507, 655) advise
redily quickly
reed advice
rekke (inf. *rekken*) care
relik(es) relic(s)
renne (inf. *rennen*) run
rente (inf. *renden*) tore
repaireth (inf. *repairen*)
  returns
repleet full
reporte (inf. *reporten*) repeat
repreeve shame
reprevable shameful
reputacioun estimation
ribaudye coarseness, filth
riden (inf. *riden*) rode
right just, quite
rightwisnesse righteousness
riot debauchery
riotour reveller, debauchee
rive (inf. *riven*) stab
Rochele La Rochelle
rolle list
rong (inf. *ringen*) rang
Ronyan see note to l. 24
Sampsoun Samson
saugh (inf. *seen*) saw
save except
se (inf. *seen*) see
see (inf. *seen*) (l. 429)
  God yow see God protect
  you

seide (inf. *seyen*) said
seint saint
seintuarie casket for relics
sely innocent
Senec Seneca
sepulture burial
sermone (inf. *sermonen*) talk
set(te) (inf. *sitten*) seated
seuretee safeguard
shape (inf. *shapen*) arrange
sholde (inf. *shullen*) should
shoop him (inf. *shapen*) planned
shortly briefly
shrewe wretch, rogue, scoundrel
shrined enshrined
shul (inf. *shullen*) shall
signes signs; (l. 605) symptoms
sires (ladies and) gentlemen
sith since; (l. 583) then
sleen kill
sleeth (inf. *sleeth*) kills
smale slim
smerte sharply
smoot (inf. *smiten*) struck
sodeynly suddenly
soghte (inf. *sechen*) searched, looked through
sondry various
soore (l. 72) disease; (l. 145) deeply
sooth true
soothe truth
soothly truly
sorwe sorrow
sory wretched; (ll. 431, 590) *with sory grace*, bad luck to you (him)
so that (ll. 90, 621, 643) so long as

soun sound
soverein principal, main
Spaigne Spain
spak (inf. *speken*) spoke, said
special particular
speken speak, say
spere spear
spicerie mixture of spices
staf stick
stal him (inf. *stelen*) stole, went secretly
sterlinges silver pennies
sterve (inf. *sterven*) die
stide (l. 667) *in stide* instead
stiked stuck
Stilboun Chilon
stirte (inf. *sterten*) jumped
stondeth (inf. *stonden*) stands
stoor livestock
stories histories
storven (inf. *sterven*) died
strenger stronger
streyne (inf. *streynen*) strain
striving strife, quarrelling
strogelest (inf. *stroglen*) strugglest
stronge (l. 503) open
stywes brothels
substaunce see note on l. 253
subtilly cunningly
suffisant competent
suffise (inf. *suffisen*) suffice, be enough
superfluitee sensual excess
suppose (inf. *supposen*) think
swere (inf. *sweren*) swear
swich(e) such
swinke (inf. *swinken*) labour
swithe quickly
sworen sworn
swote sweetly
swyn pig

taak (inf. *taken*) take
table group of Commandments
talent desire
tarie (inf. *tarien*) delay
taverner inn-keeper
thanne then
the (pronoun) thee, you
theech (inf. *theen*) may I prosper
theen prosper
theme text
ther there, where
ther-biforn previously
thider thither, there
thilke that, the same
thinketh (inf. *thinken*) it seems (e.g. *me thinketh*, it seems to me)
thise these
tho those
thoughte (inf. *thinken*) it seemed
thridde third
thurgh through
thurghout right through
thyn thy, thine
til to
to to, too
togidres together
tombesteres dancing-girls
to-night this last night
toord turd
torente (inf. *torenden*) torn to pieces
torn turn
totere (inf. *toteren*) tear apart
traitour betrayer
tresor treasure
trespas sin
trespased (*to*) offended (against)
trespasse (inf. *trespassen*) sin

trete (*of*) (inf. *treten*) deal (with)
tretee diplomacy
trewe true
trewely truly
treye three
triacle remedy
troden (inf. *treden*) stepped
trone throne, judgement seat
trouthe honour
trowe (inf. *trowen*) think, believe
tweye two
twynne (inf. *twynnen*) depart
unbokele (inf. *unbokelen*) unbuckle
unkindely unnaturally
urinals vessels for holding urine
usage habit
useth (inf. *usen*) practises, is addicted to
vanisshe (inf. *vanisshen*) waste away
verray true, real
vileynye (ll. 217, 612) wickedness; (l. 454) rudeness (but see also Appendix to *An Introduction to Chaucer*)
wafereres confectioners
war (l. 396 *be war*) beware
ware yow (*fro*) (inf. *waren*) beware (of)
warice (inf. *waricen*) heal
weel well
welked withered
wenche girl
wende (inf. *wenden*) journey
wende (inf. *wenen*) (l. 496) would have thought
wenen believe, imagine

Glossary

wey path, by-way
whan when
whennes whence
where (l. 462) whether
whilom formerly, once upon a time
widwe widow
wight person
wilfully voluntarily
winne (inf. *winnen*) gain
wise manner
wisely discreetly
wiste (inf. *witen*) knew
wit wisdom, intelligence
wives women
wol(e) will, wishes to, desires
wolde(st) would(st), wish(est)
wolle wool
wombe belly
wonder extraordinary
wonne (inf. *winnen*) gained
wont accustomed
wood mad
woodnesse madness
woost (inf. *witen*) knowest
woot (inf. *witen*) know(s)
worm creeping creature
worthy noble
wrecchednesse wretchedness
wrecches wretches
wreke him (inf. *wreken*) avenge himself
wroghte (inf. *werchen*) did, made
wrooth angry

wyke week
wyn wine
wyn-yeving giving of wine
wys wise, discreet
yaf (inf. *yeven*) gave
ybore (inf. *beren*) born
ycaried (inf. *carien*) carried
ycoined (inf. *coinen*) coined
ye (interjection) yes
ye (pronoun) you
yerne busily, rapidly
yet still
yeven give
yeven, yiven (inf. *yeven*) given
yfalle (inf. *fallen*) fallen
yfallen (inf. *fallen*) occurring
yhent (inf. *henten*) seized
yholde(n) (inf. *holden*) considered
yiftes gifts
ynough enough
yow you
ypocras drink of spiced wine
ypocrisye hypocrisy
yset (inf. *setten*) seated
yshriven (inf. *shriven*) confessed
yslain (inf. *sleen*) killed
yslawe (inf. *sleen*) killed
ystonge (inf. *stingen*) stung
yvele evil
ywis certainly, indeed